"If you don't find something inspirational ⅰ.
programming, you have ascended to the grazing range, to jui..
head bobblers of the broken stone and shattered rock variety."
  — Jon Schnepp, director of Metalocalypse, The Venture Bros.

"You wanted to build a Wonka factory in your attic but instead ended up
burning the house down. Sound familiar? If so, this book is for you. From
brainstorm, to business plan, to body and mind, Carl King has created a fantastic guide for getting the most out of your creativity."
  — Ruta Sepetys, manager of Steve Vai, LIT

"Launching your own creative career can be quite an aimless and frustrating
endeavor. This book tells you how (and why) you should do it. Bravo, Carl.
You weirdo!"
  — Jeff Friedl, drummer of DEVO, Puscifer, Ashes Divide

"Growing up, I used to think something was wrong with me. After reading
Carl's book, I now know that there is definitely something wrong with me,
and that's a good thing. If only I could beam this information back to myself
in junior high!"
  — Dan Oster, *MADtv*

"Freaks and rebels — those few that think for themselves — this book is for
you! While every other book is about how to make your creativity fit into
the world of business, this is about how to amplify your creativity into every
aspect of your life."
  — Derek Sivers, founder of CDBaby

"Like many of the people quoted on this dust-cover, I have not read Carl
King's book. I am confident, however, that my review still applies: *So, You're
a Creative Genius... Now What?* is the best book available on modern car-
tography."
  — Heather Anne Campbell, writer, *Saturday Night Live*

"This is a self-help book in the original meaning of the words. It's not teaching
you how to become a millionaire or rule the world, but effectively helps you
to create a good and solid life for yourself in an otherwise crazy and unpredictable business. You can use the advice, get started, stabilize or organize
your existing career, so you can focus as much energy as possible on the real
goal: your art!"
  — Anders Mouridsen, Los Angeles session guitarist

"I didn't think it was possible. A self-help book that is funny, brutally honest,
useful, and to the point!"
  — Dr. Astro Teller, Director of New Projects, Google

"Creativity is the most important asset we have. If you are a creative person, struggling to be the magician or the artist, you already know a lot of the things this book is telling you. However, knowing is not always enough to keep running towards your goal. This book is the mentor by your side, telling you the truth, giving you the inspiration to find the ultimate you."

— Mattias Eklund, co-founder of Toontrack / Drumkit From Hell

"In this powerful and audacious work, we recognize the creative spirit as both madder and saner than the average person, more cultivated yet more primitive. Carl's world is a kaleidoscope of thoughtful ideas and practical advice that allow us to 'reassemble' our habit-bound ways of thinking into profoundly greater personal creativity. *So, You're a Creative Genius... Now What?* is for those who dream large and aren't afraid to walk the 'side streets of life.'"

— John La Grou, TED speaker, founder of Millennia Media

"Like a bright beam of sunlight on the bookshelf horizon, King effectively guides us through what it takes to sustain creativity in an empirical but highly engaging way. Keep this book with you when your well needs water."

— Andy Alt, COO of GuitarTV / creator of The Flight 6*2 Guitar

"This book has bad news for my fellow tragically unique, pathologically shy, debilitatingly self-critical and undeniably talented geysers of creative energy. Turns out any excuse you can think of to not live your dream life daily is wholly unoriginal. There's some good news in there too, though. For instance, perhaps you are not alone in your adorable peccadillos. So let's celebrate! Party at Carl's place!"

— Barbara Ann Duffy, Animatic Editor for *The Cleveland Show* and
  Luchadora with Lucha VaVOOM

"Being creative is a lonely and silent experience most of the time. I had grown tired of chopping down trees for no one to hear. Carl's book is like a field guide to creativity... telling me I'm not alone, and to start building again."

— Frank Dreyer, executive producer, Kudelski Media and Creative

"A very inspiring book! In an age where we are overrun with flavorless information on achieving success, this is absolutely one book that no 'creative genius' can be without."

— Michael Elsner, songwriter / TV and film composer (*Hannah Montana, American Idol, High School Musical 2*)

"Carl and I went to high school together in a horrible small town in Florida. I first met him when he acted in a movie I wrote. His 'acting' consisted of mad grinning and mechanical recitation of nonsense phrases until we had to turn the camera off, weeping from exhaustion and failure. This book is proof that,

yes, weirdos from nowhere can have creative careers. Carl and I made it — and so can you."
— Chris Higgins, contributor to *The American Life* and *mental_floss* magazine

"Carl's book is chock full of practical advice — especially for creative artists to get their butts in gear. Well worth the investment!"
— Roger von Oech, author of *A Whack on the Side of the Head: How You Can Be More Creative* and *Creative Whack Pack*

"I have met many people who I'd call 'creative geniuses' — if they ever actually created something. Carl King's manual for intrepid thinkers will help them get those ideas out of their heads and into the real world where we all can see them."
— Ian Koss, publisher, *Ink 19* magazine

"If you're creative, or would like to be, Carl's book is a fascinating joy ride through the process of opening up to your complete potential. He has an amusing, complicated, and free mind which he has put to great use here. A fun read, yet a challenge to do your most creative work."
— Paul Chitlik, author of *Rewrite, A Step-by-Step Guide to Strengthen Structure, Characters, and Drama in Your Screenplay*, UCLA and Loyola Marymount University Professor, award-winning television and film writer

"Carl King's book contains great advice for an approach to life that will enhance anyone's creativity."
— Rad Sechrist, storyboard artist, DreamWorks

"This book encourages, provokes and challenges the creative person to think hard about why he creates and what the heck he's going to do about it. A must for anyone who uses his imagination and dares to make a living doing it."
— Pilar Alessandra, director of the "On the Page" Writers' Studio and author of *The Coffee Break Screenwriter*

"Carl is a focused person who is good at reminding people in creative ways that they have forgotten to write something for his book flap."
— Brendon Small, *The Brendon Small Album*

"As a middle-aged, battle-scarred veteran of the music business, reading Carl's book was like having group therapy with a large committee of old ghosts. This book provides the reader with that 'if I knew then what I know now' knowledge coupled with solid, practical advice and insight."
— Dave Meros, bassist of Spock's Beard, Eric Burdon & The Animals

"If you want to be a very successful artist like me and the author of this book, please BUY THIS BOOK and you might learn something before the end of the book!"
— Danger Woman, Autistic Singing Superhero

"Carl King has an uncanny knack for explaining both what goes on inside the creative mind and the possible frustrations that accompany that mindset. *So, You're a Creative Genius... Now What?* is filled with clever ways to channel that frustration into action that actually increases the chances of being able to have not just a passion, but a career."
— Bryan Beller, bassist of Steve Vai, Dethklok, and Dweezil Zappa

"The 21 scientists at *Scientific Proof Magazine* have proven that Carl King's book is the essential hammer of the artistic tool belt. A satellite launched, King reflects and enlightens the peripheral of the tunnel vision dreamer."
— Eman Laerton, *You Have Bad Taste In Music* and *Church Across America*

"He asked me to join an army of soldiers wearing white ski masks and declaring War On Fun, built me my very own brand of flying saucers, now a duck in a lightbulb? How can anyone say no to Carl King?"
— Marco Minnemann, famous drummer

"I've been lucky enough to have a creative career in music, television and other forms of entertainment that actually paid (most times anyway). Once in a while, a new catalyst is needed. This book got my creative magic flowing again."
— Scott Page Pagter, co-producer of *Power Rangers* / Film & TV composer / Voice & Sound Effects Director, Mattel

"Carl King is the high school guidance counselor you wish you had. King's book inspires and demonstrates how to reach your creative best, while unraveling the befuddling riddle that is the Boss Man, the client, the creative kryptonite who pays your rent."
— Zeke Piestrup, TV host, VH1 and FuelTV

"While it's true great things come in small packages, I didn't realize how true until I read *So, You're A Creative Genius... Now What?*. The power-to-weight ratio is phenomenal. So much useful information packed into so few pages. From company names to workspace theory to dealing with the agony of your own creativity, the level of helpfulness is through the roof. I wish this book had come along when I was starting my career. I might not have gone down so many dead-end paths."
— William M. Akers, author of *Your Screenplay Sucks!*

{ CARL KING }

So, you're a creative genius...

{ NOW WHAT? }

MICHAEL WIESE PRODUCTIONS

Published by Michael Wiese Productions
12400 Ventura Blvd. #1111
Studio City, CA 91604
(818) 379-8799, (818) 986-3408 (FAX)
mw@mwp.com
www.mwp.com

Cover design by MWP
Cover photographic concept by Harlan McCoy
Interior design by William Morosi & Carl King
Printed by McNaughton & Gunn

Manufactured in the United States of America
Copyright 2011 by Carl King

Library of Congress Cataloging-in-Publication Data
King, Carl M., 1975-
 So, you're a creative genius-- : now what? / Carl King.
    p. cm.
Includes bibliographical references and index.
ISBN 978-1-932907-92-6
1. Creative ability in business. 2. Vocational guidance. I. Title.
HD53.K5645 2011
650.1--dc22

                                        2011002807

Mixed Sources
Product group from well-managed
forests and other controlled sources
www.fsc.org Cert no. SW-COC-002283
© 1996 Forest Stewardship Council

This Tomato is for John Wolf.

table
of
contents

about the bubbles

throughout this book, you'll see little bubbles floating in the margins, containing baffling, contrapreneurial mantras. I promise, they're in no order at all, and might not make sense to you right now. Just put them somewhere safe for later. You never know when one of those bubbles of wisdom will pop up in your life, release its wisdom, and save you.

> Some things SHOULD be predictable. Boring, mechanical things, like doorknobs.

welcome!

instructions

this book is not for normal people.

For whatever reason, you and I have decided to follow the asymmetrical, confusing, and downright dangerous path that is a Creative Career.

I can't tell you the 1-2-3 steps to success in this. Anyone who claims he can is full of Frop. If you want the opposite of a Creative Career — a Predictable Career — just read one of the other 400,000 boring books printed this year. Maybe that one written by Dr. Whilton Popple. He has all the answers. Buy it, read it, then put it on your bookshelf and never look at it again.

Forget that guy, right?

Many of the ideas in this book are like magical spells. Sometimes the spells will work, and sometimes they won't. You might have to change the components. Try adding a spider leg, a bat tooth, or maybe a single drop of whatever was left over in Conan O'Brien's coffee mug.

It's certainly not basic arithmetic, but it's a starting point.

In a creative business, you can't always deduce what will happen if you add 2+2. So we're going to think laterally. We're going to think backwards. We're going to make some leaps into the unknown and have some fun.

One thing is certain: You're going to get unpredictable results. A Creative Career is experimental at best. The good news is that it's CREATIVE! You'll never understand it completely. It's mysterious and unpredictable, like a good science fiction movie or role-playing game.

Some things SHOULD be predictable. Boring, mechanical things, like doorknobs. Perhaps you'd rather read a book about doorknobs?

the dark side

There is also a *dark side* to this book. There's no escape. I'm not going to let you get away, because the dark side is part of the truth. I'm going to tell you about the many mistakes I've made, and the mistakes I've seen other people make.

> *"Any composition (or improvisation) which remains consonant and 'regular' throughout is, for me, equivalent to watching a movie with only 'good guys' in it, or eating cottage cheese."*
> — Frank Zappa, *The Real Frank Zappa Book*

My dark side? I've struggled with depression and anxiety for years. I've made many bad decisions. In my former life as a musician, I lost opportunities to be on my favorite albums, damaged my health, and burned bridges with my heroes.

But I'm still here, cranking out projects. Nothing can stop me.

The first commandment in setting up a top-secret laboratory is this: You must take it seriously.

If I were to write a book giving a step-by-step systematic list of rules to follow in order to be successful in a Creative Career, I'd be adding nothing of value to the world. I would be doing nothing but making the problem worse.

The truth is, there are no experts on this. There is no formula. It's not entirely controllable. This chaos will drive some to become manipulative, self-promoting whores — just so that they can make the same boring amount of money they could make at a day job.

It's a shame.

you vs. them

I wrote this book in two parts: YOU and THEM. When splitting your time between your own mad science and freelancing, it's important to put YOU first.

So that's where we're going to start.

Don't worry. Many of the "rules" will carry over to Part 2, when you'll apply everything you've learned to destroying other people's projects.

kooky reduction of concepts

In this book, you'll find a lot of numbered and bulleted lists.

Seth Godin might not approve, but I like to keep things simple and fun. There's no need to write a page of bloated text when a bullet-point list of five ideas will do. I'm not here for an extended jam session. If you want to read a sentence again, you can just rewind your eyeballs.

What works for you is not "what caters to your bad habits."

And please, don't take the lists I give as definitive. They're intended to reduce a problem to smaller, easy-to-understand parts and help you get started on your own solutions.

Sometimes there's sublime truth contained in them, but sometimes I only make them up to be funny. It's your job to figure out which is which.

Don't hurt yourself.

> *"Only sheep need a leader."*
> — Mr. Wrong, NoMeansNo, *Wrong* (Alternative Tentacles Records Virus 77, 1990)

part 1: **you**

section 1:
how to
vs.
why to

n a speech at the 2009 MWP Publisher's Summit, Michael Wiese said something along the lines of: "As we move into the era of Conscious Media, we're not asking *How To*, but *Why To*.

So before we ask *How*, we need to get to the bottom of *Why*.

Really, really, really ask yourself honestly: Is your Creative Career a recipe someone else wrote, and will you still be hungry when the cooking is done?

the rebel creator

Why do we create?

First of all, because we're *programmed* to.

Who did the programming? We don't know. God, Little Green Men, maybe MK-Ultra.

All we know is that we can't stop.

The atheistic view is that, like Howard Roark from *The Fountainhead*, we create things because we're dissatisfied with what already exists. We look around and think, "This could be *different*." We have an imagination so we can change the world. Maybe that means cleaning our bathroom. Maybe it means making a billion bucks. Maybe it means assassinating an evil dictator.

Whatever our choices, we're capable of conscious change. What an honor!

Changing the world is inherent in our nature. If you look at the earth from space, the human race is taking piles of stuff and moving it around, like ants do. You could call that a creative act, right? But over the long-term, it's transforming the planet from a green biosphere full of animals and plants into a mass of concrete, metal and plastic. If this keeps up, it's eventually going to look like a ghetto version of the Death Star. It doesn't matter if you go to Coachella and dance in the mud while Rage Against The Machine plays. We all contribute to this process of eating the earth in our own way. Until there is an alternative, we can only choose to eat slower or faster.

Many of us like to think that there is a higher purpose to all of this. A spiritual significance, or at least a fantastical future to look forward to. I'm one of those people who is more fascinated by where things are going than by where they are.

I don't know about you, but I'm sure as hell rebelling against the world I was born into. Unless you rebel in some way, you're not quite *sentient*.

We're going to have to solve these fundamental problems, and we'll only solve them with creativity. By rebelling against The Way Things Are Done.

That's right: Creativity is rebellious. Betray the tribe. It's healthy.

i might suck, but my art is great

Why do people make art?

I make it because I don't like myself. Really. I want to conjure up something that's better than me. An idealized world, a pure concept, perfection. It's an escape.

Get boo'ed off stage at least once.

I believe a lot of artists want to point to something outside of themselves and gain self-worth from it. "I might not be that thing, but darn it, *I* made it." (Ever been to a comic convention?)

I didn't choose my body or face. Through art, I can choose everything, be whoever I want to be.

Maybe what I create on purpose says more about what I believe and is more important than who I am. Or maybe what I create is what I *actually* am, because it tells the world what I believe is important; what I am at the core.

I used to think of artistic expression as a way of pointing a sign at myself. Or am I the sign, pointing at the art? Hard to tell sometimes.

the mutants vs. the normals

Normal People have plenty of books to read, plenty of fun places to go, plenty of things to succeed at. Just look at any online social network and you'll see zillions of photos of their cats and nieces and coworkers that are all amazing and brilliant and incredible. Party, party, whoo-hoo. *Yay!*

How is it that these Normals live such a carefree life, unconcerned with the psychic peril that we, the Artists — the Creative Mutants — are afflicted with?

We need to settle the score. I'm here to help YOU, The Mutant, because that's what I've always been. The Outsider. The Reject. The Alien.

Believe me, I know what it's like. No one believes in you. You can't get a job. Even your *mom* hates you.

But that makes you more interesting, right?

If you've paid attention, all of the great legends/myths/stories in the world are telling the tale of your life. All winners start out as losers, or else there wouldn't be a story to tell.

So I'm going to help you to beat Failure. I can't think of a better *Why To* than that.

what is a creative genius?

Let's not get too snobby and critical here. "Creative Genius" is a redundancy, but it's an empowering phrase! And admit it... it's something we all want to be called (at least a hundred times a day).

The word "Genius" comes from the Latin word *gignere*, which meant something along the lines of "A mystical spirit that accompanies and inspires a person to do fantastic things." Paraphrasing, but you get the point.

Think of it as being related to Genuine, Generate, and Genesis. Those are all good words, right? That makes Genius a good word, too.

Don't be shy. You can be a Genius. This isn't an I.Q. test.

Genius essentially means Creative. Commit to your Creativity, and you'll be a Genius.

Welcome to The Secret Club!

creativity's evil twin

Now that you've got an imagination, what are you going to do with it?

Let's forget about traditional definitions of words and start all over with what's important. Call it a *Helpful Delusion*.

If you use your imagination to somehow make the world better, that's Creativity.

If you use your imagination to somehow make the world worse, that's what I call *Destructivity*. It's creativity's evil twin.

Destructivity is *the imagination gone wrong.*

Examples of Destructivity:

- Convincing yourself of all the reasons you'll never succeed at this or that.
- Forcing yourself to watch the same unpleasant movies over and over in your mind.
- Finding all the things you dislike in the world and thinking about them more than the things you like.

If you haven't noticed, the world doesn't need any more help in killing us. We all get old and sick and die. So which side are you on? Why are you cheering for the other team? You've got a limited time until the Grim Reaper shows up, and he's coming for all of us.

Unless you're Ray Kurzweil, you'll eventually end up in a bed and not get back up. So why are you doing that before you're even sick?

Failure is easy. In fact, that's the default outcome of everything. If you want to fail, you already know how. Just sit back and watch TV.

Look here: Life is a struggle against being destroyed. All life forms fight to stay alive for as long as they can.

A cockroach will keep on crawling, even after you stomp on it a few times. It won't give up. Plants and animals don't know how to throw it all away. They can't make themselves miserable.

Humans seem to be the only life form on earth in hot pursuit of an "epic fail."

We love to focus on the negative.

For instance: You're walking down the sidewalk, and you see a pile of dog poop. You can get upset about it. Call your friends, complain, blog about it. Ruin everyone's day.

Or you can walk around it.

Your imagination can be used as a movie theater that plays an endless loop of worthless sounds and images. Or, you can use it to *make stuff*.

What you must do: Take control of your own imagination. Contrary to what school says, it is our most powerful tool.

inventors, explorers... madmen?

Let's make the unknown our friend.

One of the first science fiction stories was written by Johannes Kepler. It was called *Somnium* (Latin for *The Dream*). In case you don't remember, he's the guy who said:

> "The square of the orbital period of a planet is directly proportional to the cube of the semi-major axis of its orbit."

So, with that in mind, put yourself back in the 1620s. Hang out with Kepler. We're talking about the era when violins were invented, back before even Keith Richards was born. And here is this madman, writing a story about going to the moon. (And we all know it's impossible to go to the moon, because of the Van Allen radiation belts, right? OK.)

Mind your own business.

Kepler was a scientist. Or was he? Forget the label. What exactly *was* a scientist in the early 1600s? It was almost as if the role of scientist itself was undefined. Fundamentally, he was a curious mind who wanted to *understand this strange world*. So, in addition to doing a bunch of mathematics, he imagined that getting to the moon might involve making a pact with Lunar Demons and breathing through a moist sponge. Why not?

Or how about Isaac Newton, who lived a few years later? He came up with the three laws of motion and universal gravitation. He discovered "an invisible force able to act over vast distances." What? How could gravity possibly apply to the Moon the same way it applies to apples falling from a tree?

Not long before that, Galileo Galilei figured out that the planets go around the sun. His books were promptly banned for almost a hundred years, and he was locked up for the rest of his life. *Serves him right, that lunatic!*

Think about it: For the first 250,000 years of human history, the moon was a glowing thing that moved above us. We couldn't exactly say it was in the sky, because we weren't even sure what the sky was. We could only point at the glowing thing, grunt, and maybe hide from it in a cave. We didn't even know it was a sphere. Or why it seemed to change shape. Does it mean something? (A lot of people still think so.)

Feast on that chaos.

Science has become perverted into a rigid system of rules, used by atheists to make the world boring. (Ironic, considering that used to be the job of the religious fanatics.) Yet the "scientists" who discovered these truths spent their time baffled by mysteries, asking crazy questions, and using their imagination to determine what the unexpected answer might be. They didn't set out to discover *The World Is Boring.*

Losing is not more noble.

These days, our madmen are playing with Quantum Physics. They've discovered that things exist, they don't exist, they exist in two places at once, they're mostly empty space, and, hold on... now what exactly is this dark matter and what does it have to do with the Freemasons?

Ask yourself: What will be discovered in the coming years that completely destroys our current understanding of reality?

We don't know!

We're not even sure what *questions* to ask.

Example: When we were exploring the earth, discovering new continents, we didn't even know the world was round. We assumed the water went on forever and that there might be infinite world in every direction. How bizarre of a concept would that be, that if you sailed far enough, you'd end up right back where you were?

If you made that discovery, who would believe you?

Explorers are often not even entirely sure what they're trying to discover, or what they ultimately *will* discover. They just know that they want to go see *What's Over There.*

Regardless of what they expect, they often discover an answer to a question they didn't even ask.

When they return with their discoveries, the rest of the population is disappointed: they (the non-explorers) were hoping for some new way to wash their laundry or sharpen pencils!

It seems that the only people who understand that original, raw spirit of science are the New Age nuts and conspiracy theorists.

So let's keep that spirit alive. Let's not forget that progress is made by those who *aren't afraid of the unknown.*

And remember: To be able to explore, you first have to be lost.

the aliens are coming!

There is part of the human mind/soul/spirit that doesn't have everything figured out.

We spent most of our evolution/history with an incomplete map of the world. We weren't even sure who else was out there.

We'd be living in our own little universe for hundreds of years, farming and making babies... and suddenly an army of barbarians would come down from the mountains and kill everyone.

Until it actually happened, it was probably just a legend. *"They're coming! Soon!"* Everyone would laugh at the crazy old man who would rant about it. (These days, we'd call him a Militia Survivalist.)

It's probably part of our pre-conditioned psychological state as human beings. We're still expecting there to be *Others.* If we hadn't evolved to be prepared for that repeated scenario, we wouldn't have made it this far.

A large percentage of us are looking up in the sky at night, because that's where the unknown is. It's easy to point to.

How many years has it been since the Average Joe discovered something as bizarre as a manatee? There is very little left for us to find on our own planet, so we've started imagining creatures from outer space.

Thus, Science Fiction.

Imagine a beat-up old map with the edges of it filled in with what we imagine to be there: Pots of Gold. Mermaids. Dragons.

For anything interesting to happen, that's where we need to be. It's what progress is. We're here to explore. (Some of us are, anyway. The rest can all stay here and make sure we have enough staples.)

Trust your creativity forever.

helpful delusions

In this book, I'm going to introduce a lot of *Helpful Delusions*. There is nothing wrong with believing in a strange or unconventional idea if it makes the world better. Sometimes dabbling in mysticism is inspiring, and sometimes it's just a fun way to understand a problem.

Even if they're illogical, maybe you're better off believing them than not.

For those who want atheistic precision and certainty, I recommend a dictionary or encyclopedia.

are you a consumer or a creator?

I contend that if you're not actively creating something, you're not entirely alive. If a robot can do the same thing you're doing, what's the point?

Don't go through life as a Consumer.

Those fantastic people you envy (you know, the ones whose lives look like an SUV commercial) might seem like they're actively doing incredible things.

But they're not.

They're only *consuming* something you've never consumed.

They might fly to Paris and consume it. But they didn't *build* Paris. They just walk around in it. They didn't *design* that fancy car. All they do is ride in it. They don't make all that fancy wine they drink.

You want to align yourself with The Spirit Of Creativity, the guy who *makes* jewelry, not the rich guy who buys it.

If you ever get to walk around a place like Skywalker Ranch, put yourself in the mindspace of the creator. What was George Lucas thinking when he built it?

When you read a book, imagine what the author went through. Did he struggle against rejection?

If you focus on the *place* or the *product*, you're missing the most valuable lesson — the freak who built it.

As an artist, always put yourself in the shoes of the leader, the pioneer, the adventurer. Try to vibe with him. Resonate with him. Whatever New Age word fits. OK?

the hierarchy: ideas at the top

The world is a great big machine powered by Ideas.

If you follow the food chain upward, you'll always find the person with *The Idea*. Everyone else is serving that, working for him. The storyboard artist is not following his own idea, ultimately. He's doing something with a limited amount of creativity. He can be as creative as he wants until someone stops him, because someone else is paying him.

In any situation you're in, if you can get away with it, make it your goal to be the one with the ideas. You might not be the one making the most money — that's usually for Owners. But having an opportunity to be creative can be its own reward. Spending your time being creative is a privilege. (Just make sure you're not being taken advantage of.)

A technical person will always be subservient to an idea person. All technical people would be replaced with machines if they could be. Avoid being a high-level creative slave.

You want to make sure you are solving important problems. Climb the ladder of conscious, productive work. The lower you are on it, the less you are actually contributing to the world as a real, living human with an imagination.

Do work that you think is important. If you're going to spend your time working for someone else, make sure you are willing to put your own dreams and ideas aside for theirs.

> "We are the music makers, and we are the dreamers of dreams."
> — Arthur O'Shaughnessy (Ode, Music and Moonlight, 1874)

Be a dreamer. Anything else is just *shoveling*.

your mission

I believe we're all here on a mission. Caroline Myss calls it a "Sacred Contract." Some of us don't realize it. Some of us do. Our instructions come at unexpected times.

I received mine back on December 25, 1989.

I was 14 years old and at my sister's house in North Port, Florida. It was Christmas, and my mom had wrapped a brand new electric guitar and some Heavy Metal cassette tapes for me.

I was so introverted that my sister used to call me "Little Brother In a Coma." After opening my presents, I went off into the guest bedroom and sat on the bed with a boombox. One of the cassettes was *Flex-Able* by Steve Vai.

I played the tape.

The song called "Little Green Men" came on, and as I listened and read the liner notes, my future (not my past) flashed before my eyes.

I heard an internal voice say to me, *"This is what you are going to do."* As far as I know, it was the most powerful moment of my life. There were passages in the liner notes and lyrics that activated something in me:

1. "If you happen to be 'one of those people' who likes this stuff and feel yourself converting into a Steve Vai Cult-type character..."

2. "AND THERE IT IS." Why did he capitalize this sentence in the notes for "Little Green Men"?

3. "I actually believe that there are people on this planet right now, who are part of an investigative committee (let's say) for a higher intelligence. Some call them the Illuminati."

4. "The truth of the matter is that these lights, and beings, will only reveal themselves to those who are pure at heart, for these enlightened aliens leave permanent imprinted information on the psyche of those chosen humans, only to be revealed to our deteriorating planet, at the point at which our civilization will enter the new age of 'Light Without Heat.'"

5. "Hope you enjoy my Mission."

I believe this is what Michael Wiese refers to as "Conscious Media."

I didn't know what much of it meant, and I still don't. But I *felt* it. And I've been on a Mission ever since.

(Or maybe I'm the victim of brainwashing, and the *Flex-Able* album is a trigger.)

The point is, these moments of epiphany seem to be crucial. They change everything. I can't cause you to have one. I can only tell you that throughout my life, they've guided me. I do my best to *turn up the volume and listen* when they happen.

you are the one

The NeverEnding Story
Spider-Man 2
The Matrix
Star Wars
Conspiracy Theory

All of these movies tell the story of a seemingly common person accepting his true identity as The One. The guy who knows The Truth. Only nobody believes it, not even The One himself.

It can feel egotistical. Only a small step away from a "Messiah Complex."

I ran into filmmaker Kevin Smith at LAX and asked him about this.

> Me: "Do you ever feel guilty that talented people are making YOUR movie?"
> Him: "No. If they read the script and don't like it, they don't have to be in it."

See? It's OK to be The One. It doesn't have to be unhealthy.

I believe the reason that so many celebrities and rock stars are spoiled narcissists is this: They spent much of their early life suffering from a thing called Unacknowledged Talent.

End on a diminished chord.

A kid who grows up believing he'll be a rock star is most certainly delusional. He's got to be crazy to think he's one in a million — but that's exactly what works. It's what gives that Nobody the hope and audacity to become a Somebody.

> *"...The Outsider [is] a prophet in disguise — disguised even from himself — whose salvation lies in discovering his deepest purpose, and then throwing himself into it."*
> — Colin Wilson, *The Outsider*

signs from beyond

In such a confusing world, with so many options, how do you know where you're going?

I look for signs.

Coincidences. Serendipity. Impossible odds.

Want to know how and why I signed a publishing deal with Michael Wiese?

In February 2009 I read Blake Snyder's *Save The Cat!* on a whim. Bob DeRosa recommended it to me. I wasn't a screenwriter. (I honestly believed that a screenplay was a document typed up in five minutes by an intern, so that the actors could remember their lines. Smaller versions of cue cards.)

Around that time I had written a list of "100 Creative Career Mantras." I wanted to remember all of the strange lessons I've learned in my life. It was for my own personal use.

In March 2009 I formatted it as a print-ready PDF book with a cover. It was called *We Are The Pilots Of Giant Robots*.

I looked up the publishers of *Save The Cat!* and found the MWP website.

I emailed it to them.

I had no agent. No manager. No connections at all.

Within 24 hours, they wrote back and asked me to develop it into a full-length book — and they were the only publisher I sent it to!

Whoa.

A couple of months later, when it came time to sign the publishing contract, I had a lot of anxiety. *Who are these people? What do they really want from me? Do they know what is best for my ideas?*

After about a week of freaking out, I flipped through the MWP catalog. A particular product title jumped out at me:

Hardware Wars

Creativity first, business second.

<u>THE</u> *Hardware Wars*?!

I almost had to get down on the floor in my office and bow in thanks to the Gods Of Destiny.

I used to watch *Hardware Wars* (a cheap parody of *Star Wars*) on public access TV in the late '70s, before I was even in kindergarten. Michael Wiese himself had been the producer of the short student film.

What are the odds of that?

Maybe I'm nuts, but I decided right then that MWP know what they're doing. I signed, and that was that.

Sometimes, this is how the most important decisions in life are made.

the neverending story

The 1984 fantasy film *The NeverEnding Story* is a metaphor for a Creative Career — and many of the baffling, counterintuitive obstacles and challenges Creatives face. I've prepared an informal "*scriptment*" for you. (If your name is Will Akers, please don't read any further.)

Spoiler Alert!

The film tells the story of a boy named BASTIAN.

Like most protagonists, Bastian has suffered a tremendous loss. His mother (whose name is important later) has died.

Bastian is having an Existential Crisis. He wants to escape his crumbling life. He's falling behind in school. Daydreaming. Drawing unicorns.

```
BASTAIN'S DAD lectures him.

          BASTIAN'S DAD
    Get your head down out of the clouds.
    Keep both feet on the ground. Stop
    daydreaming, start facing your
    problems.
```

That's the voice of safety, conformity and mediocrity. This voice is all around us. It's there every month, telling us we need to pay the rent. It tells us to give up on our creative dreams, put on a business suit, and go to the office. Be boring, like dad.

```
On his way to school, Bastian discovers a
magical book.

          GROUCHY OLD SHOPKEEPER
    Your books are safe. Afterwards, you
    get to be a little boy again.
```

A Creative Career is a transformation. A metamorphosis. Things that once made sense lose their meaning. The Grouchy Old Shopkeeper makes it clear that things will never be the same.

```
Bastian runs off with the book, skips school,
and spends the day reading it.

The World of Fantasia is crumbling. THE
CHILDLIKE EMPRESS is dying. The people call on a
```

great warrior: a boy named ATREYU. The Childlike
Empress's representative, CAIRON, sends Atreyu on
a quest.

> CAIRON
> To save our world, no one can give you
> any advice except this: You must go
> alone, you must leave all your weapons
> behind. It will be very dangerous.

> ATREYU
> Is there any chance of success?

> CAIRON
> I do not know. But if you fail, the
> Empress will surely die, and our whole
> world will be utterly destroyed.

> ATREYU
> When do I begin?

> CAIRON
> Now.

This exchange illustrates the urgency, loneliness, and the impossible odds of our creative quest. Atreyu doesn't even know where he is going!

Lesson: Don't plan, just go.

Atreyu spends an entire week searching, without
destination. Deserts, mountains, forests. He
decides to seek out MORLA, The Ancient One, The
Wisest Being In Fantasia.

EXT. SWAMPS OF SADNESS - DAY

> BASTIAN (V.O.)
> Everyone knew that whoever let the
> sadness overtake him would sink into
> the swamp.

Atreyu trudges through the mud with his best
friend (and horse), ARTAX.

Artax stops. Atreyu tries to motivate the horse,

pulling him forward by the reigns, but it's
futile. The horse gives up and sinks beneath the
swamp.

Lesson: This is what happens to your unmotivated friends. You
can't pull 'em along. As much as you scream and beg, if they give
up, there's nothing else you can do. Accept it. They won't be going
with you.

Atreyu marches forward. He reaches his
destination and calls out for The Ancient One.

A giant turtle rises from the muck.

                  MORLA
        We haven't spoken to anyone else for
        thousands of years, so we started
        talking to ourselves.

Morla, The Ancient One, the wisest being in all of Fantasia, represents cynicism, insanity, and failure. He's that jaded old person who
hopes we give up, too. Morla has been around for so long that nothing matters anymore.

                  MORLA
        We don't even care whether or not
        we care.

Buy money, don't save it.

Morla tells Atreyu he must travel to THE
SOUTHERN ORACLE. But he'll never reach
it. It's 10,000 miles away!

Lesson: This is the voice of parents, teachers, and ho-hum fail-
ures. Why even get started? It takes years to be able to play guitar.
You'll probably never get there, right? (What we don't realize is that
it takes the same amount of time to do absolutely nothing with our
lives.)

Atreyu doesn't care. He's lost his best friend. The Nothing is
approaching. He's a warrior, so he won't give up. He'll travel on foot
if he has to.

Atreyu presses on. Growing exhausted, he fights
through the swamps.

A mighty beast called GMORK is on his trail. As
Atreyu collapses in the mud, he is saved by…

A Luck Dragon named FALKOR.

> FALKOR
> Never give up, and good luck will find
> you.

Lesson: There is no disputing the power of luck. You can either
live as a control freak in a safe, predictable universe of results that
you micromanage… or you can take some chances and see what the
world has to offer you.

Atreyu wakes up. Falkor has delivered Atreyu
to a gnome scientist named ENGYWOOK. Atreyu is
instructed on how to pass through The Two Gates,
which guard The Southern Oracle.

(There are actually Three Gates, but only two appear in the film.)

The Riddle Gate
This represents Self-Worth. Anyone who does not believe in himself
will be blasted by the death rays from the eyes of two Sphinxes. The
answer? To RUN.

The Mirror Gate
Having made it through the first gate, Atreyu must face the second.
He will encounter his true self.

> ENGYWOOK
> Kind people find they are cruel.
> Brave men discover they are cowards.
> Confronted with their true selves, most
> men run away SCREAMING.

Lesson: We wear masks in life, even to fool ourselves. To look
beneath our own masks takes courage. We find that most of our
external wars are actually internal. Our enemies remind us of ourselves, so we point and say, "That is not me."

Atreyu reaches The Southern Oracle. He finds out
that only a human child can save Fantasia. And
he can only find one beyond the boundaries of
Fantasia.

The Southern Oracle itself begins to crumble.

Desperate, Atreyu and Falkor fly off toward the hypothetical boundaries of Fantasia.

They encounter The Nothing. They are separated by a raging metaphysical storm.

Atreyu wakes up alone on a beach… and encounters GMORK.

> GMORK
> Fantasia has no boundaries. Foolish boy. Don't you know anything about Fantasia? It's the world of human fantasy. Every part, every creature of it is a piece of the dreams and hopes of mankind. Therefore, it has no boundaries. People have begun to lose their hopes and forget their dreams. So The Nothing grows stronger. It's the emptiness that's left. It is like a despair, destroying this world.

Your heroes must become your peers.

What is the purpose of The Nothing?

> GMORK
> People who have no hopes are easy to control.

Some people call this The System. The Man. The Matrix.

Be a good Cog and stay in your cubicle.

Atreyu slays Gmork. But it's too late.

The Nothing consumes Fantasia. All is lost.

Atreyu is rescued by Falkor a final time. The two fly through the void. The Nothing. They find The Ivory Tower, home of The Childlike Empress, floating on a rock.

It too will soon be destroyed by The Nothing.

In the final, heroic moment of the adventure — how can they defeat The Nothing? Simple. Bastian must become a part of The NeverEnding Story, and give The Childlike Empress a new name.

> ATREYU
> A new name? That's easy.

> CHILDLIKE EMPRESS
> Why don't you do what you dreamed, Bastian?!

> BASTIAN
> But I can't, I have to keep my feet on the ground!

> CHILDLIKE EMPRESS
> He doesn't realize he's already a part of The NeverEnding Story. He simply can't imagine that one little boy could be that important.

Bastian must accept himself and use his imagination.

Lesson: That's all? That's the secret? Yes! That's all there is to creativity.

> CHILDLIKE EMPRESS
> Call my name! Bastian, please! Save us!

> BASTIAN
> Alright! I'll do it! I'll save you! I will do what I dream!

Bastian runs to the window and shouts into a raging storm.

> BASTIAN
> Moonchild!

(Yes, apparently his mother's name was Moonchild.)

Everything goes black.

> BASTIAN
> Why is it so dark?

> CHILDLIKE EMPRESS
> In the beginning, it is always dark.

Lesson: Our old friend, Writer's Block, makes an appearance.

The Childlike Empress presents Bastian with a single glowing grain of sand. All that is left of Fantasia.

> THE CHILDLIKE EMPRESS
> Fantasia can arise in you. In your dreams and wishes, Bastian. What are you going to wish for?

> BASTIAN
> I don't know.

> THE CHILDLIKE EMPRESS
> Then there will be no Fantasia, anymore.

> BASTIAN
> How many wishes do I get?

> THE CHILDLIKE EMPRESS
> As many as you want. And the more wishes you make, the more magnificent Fantasia will become.

Be able to make sacrifices.

> BASTIAN
> Really?

> THE CHILDLIKE EMPRESS
> Try it.

She's right. Try it.

the imagination

Our minds are made for doing two things:

1. Seeing things that are there.
2. Seeing things that are not there.

Which ability is the more glorious and noble?

The Imagination is the most powerful tool we have, yet it's the least nurtured, the least developed. In school, we're judged not by what we can create, but by how much we can *memorize*. If you look

21

at the thirteen-year K-12 arc, what's the story? *Our imagination is slowly beaten out of us and replaced with facts.*

Each of us owns the most powerful tool in the universe — we can imagine *anything*.

So why write a screenplay full of normal people, mediocre jokes, and a predictable ending? Why program your computer to play simple 4/4 drumbeats? Why go somewhere you've already been a zillion times?

Enjoy what you are doing, or don't do it right now.

Don't let your tombstone read:

"Here lies Bob, who spent the majority of his waking hours running a cash register."

If you're reading this book, you're better than that.

without question

"You can't connect the dots looking forward. You can only connect them looking backwards."
— Steve Jobs, Stanford University Commencement Speech, 2005

What do you jump into without question? Not many things in life.

Are you ready? With creativity, you've got to jump right into the process and drown in it before you can figure out where you're going. Otherwise you'll be calculating too much, and what you create will be superficial.

Stop second-guessing yourself and trying to figure out how others are going to react to your art.

Art is best when it's *challenging*. Artists are too obsessed these days with making everything immediately digestible and profitable, out of fear of obscurity and failure.

Be brave. Make something substantial. Something that requires multiple viewings. Make those lazy consumers burn a few extra calories watching your video.

This is not fast food. Art is important!

let's define success and failure

"It is impossible to win a war with no criteria for success."
— Unknown

Everyone has their own definition of *Success* and *Failure*.

Sure. You can define success however you want, and it might make you feel accomplished. Every phase of a project can be completed successfully. But that doesn't mean the project is successful.

Within the context of a Creative Career, success means *"Exponential Return On Creative Investment."*

Success IS NOT:
- Steve Vai took me out to lunch when I moved to Los Angeles.
- My record got great reviews in *Decibel, Kerrang!* and *Modern Drummer.*
- Jon Schnepp from *Metalocalypse* likes my cartoon idea.
- Roger Von Oech wrote a blog about me.
- Mike Portnoy of Dream Theater bought my CD.

Success IS a Creative Career project that:
- Reaches its intended audience.
- Pays its creator. With money. Real money, right now. As in, it's already been deposited and you bought groceries with it.
- Funds the next Creative Career project.

If you use the phrase *"I'm getting a lot of positive reactions,"* you know you're doomed.

are you well-adjusted?

I've met a lot of people in my zillions of years in the Creative Business — some successful, some not. Some of them are happy and some of them are miserable. I haven't found any correlation to their amount of "success."

Producer Brendan Davis turned me on to this idea: No matter where anyone is on their career path, they MUST be well-adjusted to it.

Think of failure as a desert that must be crossed.

The way you deal with "failure" will determine how you deal with "success." In other words, once it comes to you, if you typically deal with failure inappropriately, you will also deal with success inappropriately. You will end up right where you started after being given a single break.

From what I have learned, failure really means *"unable to effectively respond to problems and difficulties as they arise."*

All people with talent and motivation will encounter roughly the same hardships as everyone else throughout their Creative Career path. There is not just one single failure that will determine everything.

Failure is a habit, not an event.

Adjust yourself to it well.

journey & destination

Are Journey and Destination equally important?

Sure, part of your outcome (the value you create in the world) can be the process itself. The actions you take are part of your life. You experience them.

Consider that how you get there can be as important as where you are going.

But what is the net result? What if your Journey is honorable, but your Destination is worthless?

Example: If you're doing creative work for an uncreative company (graphic design department for cluster bombs to be dropped on innocent kids), *what's the point?*

On the other hand, is it possible to completely remove yourself from the grid? Probably not. You'll always be part of the system. Someone is probably doing something you don't approve of while listening to the music you wrote.

> *"No matter what you do, you're always workin' for the man."*
> — Hellworms, *"Zillionaire," Crowd Repellent* (Alternative Tentacles Records, 1998)

You can only make the best choices in your own life.

the story of change

All life is the story of change, from one state of being to another.

Everyone moves through time and space, becoming. Or unbecoming.

Here's my story:

I was in high school for five years. I learned to drive when I was 20. I lost my virginity when I was 28, and could never seem to keep a girlfriend. I was overweight (225 pounds) and depressed (going to therapy). I lived with my mom until I was in my 30s.

Out of that poor excuse for a *curriculum vitae*, I'd like to highlight one particular change... one adventure from Point A to Point B.

When I was 20 years old, I was washing dishes at a filthy all-night diner in South Venice, Florida, walking back and forth to work in the rain. There was one small speaker in the ceiling that would play '70s funk. One night, in between my assignments to clean the toilets and scrape scum out from under the floor mats, the manager approached.

He asked me to change the marquee out front to say "Steak and Eggs" — and he took his time spelling it out on paper for me, expecting me to be that stupid.

> **Be a Pro, or be a Hobbyist. Don't be an Amateur.**

Here I am, 15 years later, writing a whole book.

Take that, restaurant manager. (And take that, younger version of me who didn't believe in himself.)

refuse to accept your current situation

If you want to change, you must *refuse to accept your current situation*. Don't take it seriously. It's not real.

(That's another Helpful Delusion.)

On a day-to-day basis, it's too easy to get sucked into the world that is projected all around you. The dramas, the people, the bad ideas.

If you want to move away from that bad part of town, don't become part of it. Keep it external from yourself, like it's a movie.

bow & arrow

In January 2010, I went to NAMM in Anaheim. It's a big music industry convention.

We interviewed Mr. Paul Reed Smith, the man behind PRS Guitars, played by Carlos Santana, Ted Nugent, Rush, Primus, Opeth, etc.

We asked him... what started it all?

After a thoughtful pause, he said:

> *"Not being allowed to have good gear... All the guys in the neighborhood, they had good gear, their parents bought them good gear. But nobody in my house bought me anything... Not being allowed into somebody's club will drive the bus pretty well."*

I call this the **Bow & Arrow**.

The trick is to see how far you can pull yourself back (or get pulled back by someone else) without snapping the bowstring.

The farther you can pull it back without breaking it, the farther the arrow will travel.

This is an analogy for storytelling and adventure. Great men and women throughout history are often pulled back by something before they launch forward. Where the arrow is coming from is as important as where it is going. If you look closely enough, you can often find that initial tension that created all of the forward motion.

My bowstring came dangerously close to snapping in mid-2006. Had I not capitalized on that potential energy, I believe my Creative Career would have been over. Luckily, it shot me 3,000 miles across the country at Los Angeles.

the cargo cult

During World War II, American and Japanese armies built military bases on islands in the Pacific.

The native people would watch planes land, unload cargo, and take off again. To them, it appeared to be a magical ritual. Supplies came down from the sky on giant birds. Medicine, food, clothing. *Gifts from heaven!*

Get out of that small town. Then go back.

After the war ended, the islanders built their own bases: airplane towers, coconut headphones, and even life-size airplanes — hoping that if they imitated the behavior of the soldiers, the cargo would come.

Before you laugh at those silly islanders, ask yourself:

Isn't the world just one big Cargo Cult?

I've found that the entertainment industry is a contrived process of reverse-engineering success. One guy writes that magical hit song, and forever after, millions of people try to replicate its success. They put on the sunglasses, silly boots, mess up their hair, and think it will *Fool The Gods*. They even write books about it, and try to turn it into college degrees.

For the most part, it doesn't work. Why?

"Hits" occur spontaneously, in a reactive, organic environment. They used to just happen; now they are *made* to happen. Still, no one knows when they actually *will* happen.

It's like trying to get struck by lightning. You can do your best to position yourself under the dark clouds, climb a stone tower, and raise a fancy hammer in the air while screaming "Thor!"

But scientists can't even agree on how lightning is formed.

Good luck.

the three acts of your creative career

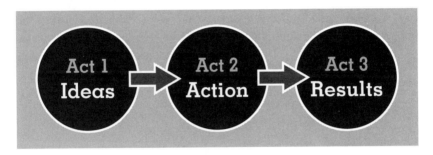

The Three-Act Structure of storytelling is a convenient framework for understanding the arc of your Creative Career.

It's common to be in different phases with different career paths at once, and it can apply to each individual project.

Act One: Ideas

This Act usually starts early in life, although it can happen at any age. Maybe you were inspired to pick up a musical instrument. You might not even be sure why; you were just drawn to it. It's good to follow your intuition in this Act.

> *"Follow your bliss."*
> — Joseph Campbell

Example: I got into graphic design because I walked into a print shop one day and loved the smell of paper and ink.

The problem: Too many talented people get into this phase and never leave.

Act Two: Action

This phase is not just action, but *meaningful* action. This is where you get serious, make sacrifices, and commit to your path. You're not just frantically trying random things, guided by inspiration. You're making calculated (often drastic) moves to improve your situation. You've realized how much of your energy you've spent on things that go nowhere. It's time to get serious.

Example: I didn't want to spend my whole life in a small town in Florida, so I moved to Los Angeles.

The Problem: Action isn't enough.

Act Three: Results

In this act, you finally get some results. You figured out the magical combination, found a market for what you do, and started hitting the bull's-eye. Money probably appears. Welcome to the rest of your life.

My mindset is this: Nothing before Act Three counts. Until you get results, you haven't really done anything. You can say, "But it's practice!" Practice for what? Failing? Results are the best practice you can get.

Don't honk. Tell a good story.

section 2:
the
creative
career
process

the four archetypes

In writing my 2005 book, *How To Sell The Whole F#@!ing Universe To Everybody... Once And For All!*, I spent some time studying the basics of Hermeticism. As others have, I found a lot of meaning in the first two cards of The Tarot: The Fool and The Magician. I won't go into a lot of mystical bulldada here, but I use these archetypes because they represent the path we are on toward a Creative Career. Doing stuff on Earth: making "something" out of "nothing" through Willpower.

Sure, maybe it's Satanic — the kind of stuff you'd find Aleister Crowley talking about with his buddies over a chess game. Controlling the universe? Sounds scary. But it's what we're all doing here, and there's no escape. So let's try to do it from a good place.

The Businessman

- Just wants to turn $1 into $2. Is that so wrong?
- Is competitive.
- Takes the initiative.
- Always shows up early.
- Is Conscious Mind oriented.
- Is guided by Logic and Reason.
- Has an atheistic view of the material world.
- Focuses on skills (learned abilities).
- Is organized.
- Socializes in order to advance his career.
- Takes advantage of The Fool and The Artist.
- Wants to control.
- Likes mechanics and workflow.
- Corresponds to Left-Brain Thinking.
- Keyword: Rich.

Learn to say no.

What is that "something" that The Businessman is making out of "nothing"? Usually, it's money. Not necessarily because they're greedy bastards, but because it's a system that is simple to understand and count. Things go in a specific order, you work through a series of steps, and you get the result. Done! It's like playing World of Warcraft. You follow the directions on the screen and you get Gold. There's not much mystery to it. It's a predictable life.

The Businessman doesn't understand why The Artist can't just put A, B and C in sequence and succeed like he can. Why doesn't that dirty-haired slacker get his act together?

The Artist

- Is a dreamer.
- Spends a lot of time contemplating meaning.
- Will NEVER show up on time.
- Doesn't care about money. Always broke.
- Has no sense of urgency.
- Draws inspiration from his subconscious.
- Wanders.
- Is guided by emotions.
- Focuses on talents (inherent abilities).
- Is superstitious.
- Is disorganized.
- Wants to escape from this mundane universe.
- Is inspired by chaos.
- Corresponds to Right-Brain Thinking.
- Keyword: Famous.

Live up to the hype.

Artists don't like this world. Why? Because the one in their heads is better. Artists tend to be idealists. They're also notorious for destroying their bodies. But you know what? Artists are the ones who come up with the weird ideas The Businessman turns into a formula.

The Fool

- Has no goals in life.
- Does not question authority.
- Follows the crowd.
- Is always looking to someone else for advice.
- Will be an employee forever.
- Surrounds himself with anyone who likes him.
- Does not consider long-term consequences.
- Doesn't care what anything means.
- Is not interested in learning or developing.
- Seeks immediate gratification.
- Is drawn toward passive recreation.

- Consumes more than he creates.
- Blames others for his failure.
- Corresponds to No-Brain Thinking.
- Is the victim of The Businessman.

This is the bulk of the human race. Why? Because everyone starts out as The Fool. We all know what it's like. The way it works out, most stay there. If we evolve at all, we generally become either The Businessman or The Artist — turning toward one side or the other.

The Magician

- Learns to balance creativity and self-discipline.
- Understands the parallels between art and commerce.
- Draws upon his conscious AND subconscious mind.
- Answers his own questions, or asks the right people.
- Learns many skills and develops his talents — he values them both.
- Is a collector of wisdom and great art.
- Is a wrangler of talented people.
- Is focused on results.
- Accepts that nothing is perfect.
- Has a holistic view of give and take.
- Enjoys the journey AND the destination.
- Is an inspiration to both Businessmen and Artists.
- Corresponds to Whole-Brain Thinking.
- The Fool can't even conceive of what The Magician is.

Who Are These Magicians?

Kevin Smith
Steve Vai
Frank Zappa
George Lucas
John La Grou
Matt Groening
Danny Elfman
Dave Weckl
Ayn Rand

These are people who (as far as I can tell) figured out how to balance art and business. It doesn't mean all of them became rich and famous, but they've each embodied that Elusive Paradox of Duality.

Now remember that these archetypes don't directly translate into PROFESSIONS. These are more like *personality types*.

For instance, I know many working musicians who embody The Businessman archetype. Imagine a guy who practices his instrument, learns the songs, shows up on time, and has great gear. But most of his Artist tendencies died long ago. He never writes his own songs. You can count on him to be a solid machine, but if you're looking for an adventurous player who has a unique voice, you'll get that (and a slew of other unsolvable problems) from The Artist.

You might also think an animator is an Artist. While it does require an essential visual talent, much of animation is calculated and strict — following the laws of physics. It is akin to programming a piece of software, and requires disciplined, linear thinking. Most of the creativity happens during writing and storyboarding. After that, it's a matter of executing the blueprint.

In most any profession out there you'll find examples of every archetype. You'll find most medical doctors are The Businessman archetype (and hopefully not The Fool). I'm sad to say I've met only a few who are The Magician. The same goes for school teachers, auto mechanics, and politicians.

Of course, these Mythological Categories aren't supposed to define every aspect of a person's existence. That's what we have astrology for, right?

Here's a personal example that shows the difference between Artist and Businessman very well:

When I was 20, I played in a local punk rock band.

Our guitarist was The Businessman. He was always on time, had practiced his parts, his guitar was in tune, and he had good gear. He had a dark sense of humor and unusual ideas for songwriting. His guitar playing was about average, but sometimes he struggled to keep up. He was rational, dependable, and took the band seriously. He was solid. He had what you'd call "high standards for organizational skills."

After some personal disagreements between the guitarist and the drummer, we kicked the Businessman out and got an Artist to play guitar.

The Artist didn't know the names of the chords (or even the names of the guitar strings), but he could play any song on the radio flawlessly after hearing it only once. Music was a natural language for him. He could somehow visualize any piece of music on his guitar neck. He had an uncanny ear and a photographic aural memory, since he had been playing music since he was three years old. But when it came time for band practice, The Artist was nowhere to be found. I often had to go out around town looking for him. When we performed, he'd often stop in the middle of a song and play cover songs that no one else recognized. He was really in his own world, but he played with a lot of energy and enthusiasm. He was always having fun, and always *smiling*!

Do not resent the incompetent.

If you could somehow combine the best of those two into one superhuman guitarist, he'd end up on the list of Magicians. But unfortunately, it's nearly impossible to find those two elements in one place. It's as if they're mutually exclusive. Anyone who has them both is probably already successful.

the man with two brains

I've read a few books. They say we have two brains in one.

Tradition and myth say it's half-and-half. Two hemispheres doing different things. Some say it's like two computers, one of them processing linearly and the other laterally.

Others split us up into Heart and Mind. In the 1970s, Rush made a concept album about that one called *Hemispheres*, which tells the story of humanity by correlating the two halves of the brain to Greek gods (Apollo and Dionysus).

I recommend that you check out *Whole-Brain Thinking: Working From Both Sides of the Brain to Achieve Peak Job Performance* by Jacquelyn Wonder.

I've found that there are too many pseudo-scientific arguments floating around out there. I've never cut up a brain in a laboratory, but I have used one for thirty-five years.

So I'm going to join in on the fun and say it's 29% conscious and 71% unconscious. (Because I have a thing for prime numbers, and none of this is worth arguing about, anyway.)

Let's imagine that your brain is a limousine.

The part of your brain you can control is the limo driver. He sits up front and looks at the road, swerves in and out of traffic. So he's in control, right? He's got his hands on the steering wheel, his feet on the gas and break pedals. He opens doors, carries luggage, reads maps, gets you there on time.

But he doesn't decide where to go, does he? He gets his instructions from the rock stars who are partying in the back. But he can't see them, because the tinted window is up. The guy up front is only doing his job, making things work right.

He knows WHERE he is going, but not WHY he is going.

In my experience, the greatest ideas come from the back of the limo. That 71% that slips through the tinted glass. Why would you want to throw away 71% of your resources?

You can call it God, or a Muse, or Inspiration, or The Infinite Chaos Generator Between Your Ears. It doesn't matter.

Remember, we're after Results.

get the broad strokes right

Focus on the big picture. Don't spend all of your time on the fine details. Great big ideas are simple. If your broad strokes are wrong, the smaller details won't matter.

everything is a haiku

Who thinks Haiku poetry is too formulaic? I don't.

For those who don't know, it's a form of Japanese poetry. Here's the formula:

The first line has five syllables.
The second line has seven syllables.
The third line has five syllables.

And that's it! That's all you get. Work with it!

Here is my favorite Haiku, written by an old friend of mine, Captain Coppertop, and inspired by a scene in *History of the World, Part 1* by Mel Brooks.

> *Oedipus walks by.*
> *I recognize and greet him.*
> *"Hey, Motherf#@!er."*

Brilliant. Why?

First, the final word in line three delivers the surprise punchline, correlating to the first word in the poem. (Oedipus is a Greek hero who accidentally married his own mother.)

Second, because "Hey, Motherf#@!er" is an informal greeting, as mentioned in line two. Third, he's contrasted modern slang with ancient Greek mythology. We've got the highbrow and the lowbrow. It's stylistically ironic.

Every line in this poem is meaningful and contributes to the forward momentum. Omit one of the lines and it falls apart.

Let's try a variation:

> *Oedipus walks by.*
> *I recognize and greet him.*
> *"You are Oedipus."*

It's got no surprise twist or ironic ending. It just ends exactly how you say it's going to end. The rules of Haiku have been followed, it's 5-7-5, it all makes sense, but there's no drama, tension, punchline. (This is the equivalent of listening to J.S. Bach, in my opinion.) The final line (and preferably the final word) MUST be meaningful and unexpected, because that's where everything lands.

Here's one more try:

> *Oedipus walks by.*
> *I recognize and greet him.*
> *"You are my dentist."*

That's an *Adult Swim*-style *non sequitur* and it's silly, but it's not as brilliant as "Hey, Motherf#@!er," because it's only unexpected and not meaningful. Dentist has nothing to do with Oedipus.

Now here's the point of this: The words wouldn't be as interesting if the author wasn't confined to the strict syllable count that Haiku provides. You wouldn't get that same feeling of, "It's so clever that he made it all fit into 5-7-5."

It's the same in the following arts:

- Western Tonal Music is limited to 12 notes.
- Most music you've heard is written with the same 3 chords.
- Most movies you've seen are shown in 3 acts.

- Screenplays are printed in 12-point type on white paper.
- Most sentences end with a period or a question mark.
- Computer monitors use 3 colors (red, green and blue) to display millions of colors.
- Basketball players fight over a single ball. If you just gave them both a ball, there would be no game.

Limitations make life interesting. They're not meant to be a stamp-stamp-stamp cookie cutter. They're the boring parts that make the clever parts what they are.

> **Be specific when you promote yourself.**

Without them, there would be nothing for the playfulness to rebel against. Rules really are made to be broken.

But it's impossible to be 100% unique and break all of the rules.

Just decide which elements of your work that you want to be predictable. Keep a few things traditional, then break everything else. As weird as they are, even Sleepytime Gorilla Museum have songs that stop and start, CDs to sell, and a website to visit. They drive around the country and play on stages, for audience, who applaud.

If I type the phrase "The entire earth bulged and exploded like a toilet full of hot dogs," I am still using formal sentence structure to convey a convoluted and strange idea. I am typing in English. You are reading it in a book or on a computer screen, which is a standardized tool.

There is only so weird you can be.

I've heard it said that jazz music is drawing a circle on the floor, keeping one foot in it, and then seeing how far outside you can dance around with the other foot before bringing it back in.

Try to do that with your own art. Ask yourself what you can "break" to make your work interesting. Do it in the same way repeatedly… and Congratulations! You now have your own style.

what makes strong art?

You can argue with this all you want. If you don't like it, write your own list.

Here are seven distinct elements that apply to most art forms.

1. **It has Conflict.** Both Consonance And Dissonance. There needs to be a struggle of some kind. Two opponents, and one you can root for.

2. **It has a Foreground and a Background.** Something is in focus, something is out of focus. The lead instrument and the accompaniment. Your eyes/ears should be drawn toward one thing and away from everything else. A single focal point at any given time.

3. **It has Contrast.** Light, dark. Big, small. Loud, soft. Fast, slow. Ugly, pretty. Square, circle. Happy, sad. Opposites enhance.

4. **It has Direction.** Strong art shows motion of some kind, from one of the above extremes to another. Before, after. Take the audience on a journey, from one place to another.

5. **It has Surprise.** If you want to make the same old stuff every day, go work in a factory.

6. **It Makes a Statement.** In *A Hitchhiker's Guide To The Galaxy*, Douglas Adams concluded that "The Ultimate Answer to the Ultimate Question of Life, the Universe, and Everything" is... 42. The philosophical premise being: *If you do the math, the world we live in doesn't make sense.*

Most importantly:

7. **It Affects People.**

If it doesn't, it's dead.

Why go through all the trouble of making something, if no one is interested in it?

Notice I used the word "Strong" instead of "Good."

In most cases, the more of these elements your art has, the better off it will be.

the secret to making weak art

If there is one secret to making weak art, it is to *ignore your dark side.*

Art is therapeutic and sometimes less expensive than counseling.

Embrace your mental malfunctions, your past pain, things you don't like — just draw from it all and go!

permission to be creative, sir

Don't worry. You don't need to join a union or pay $8,000 to go to a conference in Long Beach.

You're pre-approved!

Amateurs go to workshops and get discouraged, because they're bombarded by a long list of reasons they'll always suck. All of the professional jargon, tricks, secrets and insider tips are diversions to keep them out.

Don't trust the *faux*-Pros. Anyone can study and learn technique. The hard part is coming up with great ideas in the first place.

If you investigate those who have "succeeded," more often than not you will hear them say, "I had no idea what I was doing. I just started doing it."

In other words, they succeeded because they didn't know they couldn't. They came up with a great idea and sold it on their first try.

So why worry about distribution, budget, and audience? These are external things that are not central to expressing a creative idea.

I can't even count how many times I have heard of someone "developing a project." What they mean is that they're just waiting for the funding or approval to come through. Then it doesn't and they throw the idea away.

Why can't we express an idea without having permission, budget, funding, all this *nonsense*?

If your idea is truly great, you will not abandon it. You will not let the suits get in your way. You will express your creative ideas. You'll make them happen.

Even if you have to draw them on the backs of business cards, like Hugh MacLeod [*gapingvoid.com*] did.

talent vs. skill

For a successful Creative Career you need both Talent and Skill — and you need to know the difference between them.

Talents are things that come easily to you.

Skills are things you work hard at to balance against your talents.

Talent is the central core. There is no substitute for it. Skill is added later. "Jacuzzi-style," as Eman Laerton says.

The problem with talent is that it's often invisible to the person who has it. Since, by definition, talent is effortless ability. *We think that in order to be good at something, it should be hard for us to do.*

Big mistake!

The problem with skill is that talented people neglect it, and rely on their talents as a crutch. They don't bother to develop skills because their talent came to them so easily. We like things that are easy, don't we?

If you don't accept and apply your talents, you'll be cursed throughout your Creative Career. You will not only be working uphill against yourself, you will be competing against people who are naturals.

And if you don't develop skills, you'll be a *one-trick pony*.

Everyone has talents. It's just a matter of discovering them. That's why you should try many things. It's also possible to be multitalented, just so you know. In fact, it's quite common.

Find out what you're good at, and become excellent at it.

Find out what you're bad at, and become mediocre at it.

It's the professional thing to do.

collaboration/partners

"There is no God greater than the God of Creativity.
All lesser gods must be sacrificed in his name."
— Pastor Eman Laerton

If you're going to work with someone on a creative project, define your roles. Clearly, explicitly, even brutally. Let there be no misunderstanding about who has the final say over what.

I don't recommend 50/50 ownership of anything.

Friends are one thing. Business partners on a finite project are another. Don't get them mixed up.

There is nothing wrong with being the benevolent dictator.

am i too old? too young?

A Creative Career is a lifelong commitment.

If you're going to do this, you need to Trust Your Creativity Forever. Believe in your ability to consistently create new ideas in the future. *Commit.*

Life expectancy is 80 years. Yet many people grow old and worn out at 30. Why? One-third of the way into life is a terrible time to stop being creative.

Work in a vacuum.

John Williams composed the *Star Wars* soundtrack when he was 45 years old.

As you learn and grow older, you should be collecting high-level lessons. You should be evolving away from physical labor and toward mental labor. You will eventually get paid, not for carrying heavy rocks, but for your wisdom regarding where to place them.

Start as a PA, end as a Producer.

It doesn't matter how old you are. You can re-invent yourself at any time. Don't worry about the guilt of changing your path and doing what you really want to do at any point in your life, because what you want to do will change over time.

If you've already written one 5,000-page book about Social Metaphysics, maybe one is enough. Don't look back at what you've done and measure yourself against it. Move on and try new things that stimulate you and make your life an *adventure*.

We all have a limited time here, in this strange room called Life, and we'll eventually not be in it anymore. So we may as well do as much as we can before we go, whether we're young or old.

launch it into space

As soon as you start making stuff, *release it!*

You want to start getting feedback from your audience *right away*. Don't be afraid of input. Share your ideas with others in order to gain outside perspectives. Maybe someone will find a flaw in your idea or see it in a new way you hadn't thought of.

You're not obligated to take their advice.

The great thing about working with digital media is that you can update your work at any time. As you get better every day, you have the option of fixing your mistakes.

The important thing is this: It's out there.

A lot of improbable things can and will happen. You never know who is watching, or where that single MP3 file might end up.

Many years ago, I mailed a free CD to some kids in Chicago. Four years later, one of them got a job working for rock guitar virtuoso Steve Vai. Another four years later, I was having lunch with Steve Vai.

Who knows... maybe in another four he'll let me wash his car!

put yourself on the world showcase

At some point in your creative development, you're going to need to "stand alone against the whole world," as Ayn Rand said in *The Fountainhead*.

The sooner, the better.

I've come up with this concept called The World Showcase. All it really means is this: Publish your work in a highly-visible place, where it will be measured according to the standards of the most talented and creative and motivated people in the world.

You *want* your work to be compared to that of The Masters. (You know, those people who have zillions of fans and zillions of dollars and zillions of mental problems.)

You've got to get over the fear of not being good enough, and there is only one way through it. So go for it.

If you suck, you'll learn that much faster.

compare your work to the best

Always have a reference. When you're working on a piece of music, have something on hand to compare it to. A/B it.

Make sure your art is in good company. If you listen to good music all day, your music will get better. Calibrate your sense of quality.

If you're recording a metal album, put it up against Pantera.

Does it sound as good? No? Then *fix it*.

You can use critical thinking and problem solving to find out what your recording is lacking. Train yourself to hear the difference.

But don't worry: Someone else's art will always look better than yours, because it's got that exotic magic.

taking criticism

All feedback and criticism is constructive. If you write a screenplay and the reader has a question, it means you didn't do your job.

"The reader is always right."

The two goals of taking criticism:

1. Improving your work.
2. Improving your work.

As unpleasant as it can be, without feedback and criticism, you will never know what works and what doesn't.

So let's define "what works."

Your first goal is to get people to pay attention.

Rule One in Carl King's Guide To Successful Communication: *If you can't learn how to control people's eyeballs, you're screwed.*

The only way you're going to learn that is by sticking things in front of those eyeballs and finding out what happens. What did they see? How long did they look at it? What made them stop?

Examples:

If you want to be a comedian, start by writing a hundred jokes. Someone, somewhere, will laugh at one of them. Figure out why it worked. Write a hundred jokes like that one. Maybe only two of the next batch are funny. Progress!

If you want to be a musician, play your music for your mom. (Just kidding. NEVER do that.) Play your music for someone you don't know. Check out the reaction. Did they get "into" it emotionally? If they don't, you're dead. On the other hand, if they nod their heads and want to purchase some form of alcohol, move to Los Angeles, because you've been CHOSEN.

If you want to be a screenwriter, kidnap a musician (he deserves it, for all the MySpace band spam he sent out in 2006), tie him to a chair, shine a light in his face, and make him read your elegant screenplay in front of you. (It's the only way you can simulate the emotional state of a professional reader in the film industry.) Watch every visible reaction. Did he laugh at anything? Did he get confused and have to go back? Did he get the characters mixed up? Does he beg for an alternate form of physical torture?

Accept ALL criticism from the poor bastard. When you untie him, thank him for letting you ruin his day.

good news: no one cares

The good news is that unless you're already succeeding, no one is going to care what you write/record/publish/draw/perform/say. Enjoy the artistic freedom of obscurity!

If you want to start a blog, don't overthink it. You don't need to worry about a strong premise or theme. It helps to get beyond the initial pressure of feeling like everyone is going to scrutinize everything you do.

The truth is, if anyone is even reading it, you're doing something right. That's called a *Good Problem*.

I see the same thing with bands who want to put out their first record. They act like it's the only one they'll ever make. It's life or death. "The whole world is watching!"

No, it's not. It's watching a video of a cat playing with an iPad.

If you're going to be committed to it for the long-term, you've gotta just start releasing stuff, and have that be a normal process. Lose your virginity and start publishing so it won't be a big deal anymore. Get comfortable with how that feels.

Hold onto this paradox:

1. This is the big one, and
2. This is just another thing I do.

> *"The test of a first-rate intelligence is the ability to hold two opposed ideas in the mind at the same time, and still retain the ability to function. One should, for example, be able to see that things are hopeless and yet be determined to make them otherwise."*
> — F. Scott Fitzgerald

a culture of critics

TV shows like *American Idol* are creating a culture of snobby, critical, mean people who love to watch other people fail.

Art is not about competition. It's about self-expression. Let's never forget that.

Focus on results.

People are quick to predict what won't work. "The title is too long." "People will be alienated by the words Outer Space." "That shirt just doesn't fit with your pre-existing meme." *We're all armchair marketers, aren't we?*

If you listen to that crap, you might never make or release anything.

creating the ultimate supervillain

Do you want everyone to like you? Time to get over that.

Circa 2005, I became a First-Class Internet Troll.

I'd travel around from message board to message board, *stirring up problems.*

I'd create multiple accounts. I'd think of one as The Villain, and the other would be The Hero. Each would have its own persona and backstory.

The Villain would write long, formal, opinionated essays. The Hero would use slang and argue against him, representing the voice of the average message board user. The Villain was an elitist intellectual, and also happened to be a musician, with a new album.

People took sides.

To get attention for my arguments, I used a trick I called "Wounded Bird." I would intentionally leave logical errors in The Villain's arguments, to encourage people to attack him. It engaged the readers and caused them to take action. They couldn't help themselves — everyone wants to be right, to win an argument, to defeat someone.

What they didn't realize is that The Villain was smarter than he let on. He'd unravel yet another brilliant argument with barely noticeable flaws. They'd attack again. It was like Martial Arts against preschoolers. *"Come on... hit me!"*

What was my goal? I wanted to make people take an *action*, whether it was positive or negative. I liked to watch them try to argue with someone who didn't really exist. Much more fun than video games.

The secondary effect was that it helped me sell my albums, released under the name of The Villain, which was Sir Millard Mulch.

Some of the smarter readers would pick up on the game and become fans. Most never got the joke. I was an online version of personas like Borat, Neil Hamburger, or Tony Clifton... but before I knew they existed.

In 2006, I changed the name of Sir Millard Mulch to Dr. Zoltan Øbelisk, moved to Los Angeles, and shot a series of low-budget political speeches making fun of popular bands.

I wore a wig and sci-fi glasses, made strange faces, and waved my arms around in gestures like I was directing an airplane or trying to breakdance. Dr. Zoltan used no contractions, and always spoke in a formal voice. No slang. No Fun. (In fact, he declared War On Fun.)

I posted the videos on YouTube, and between everything (Sir Millard Mulch and Dr. Zoltan) I ended up with somewhere around half a million views, most of them violently upset music fans. A great return on investment, because these people were paying very close attention to my videos. Not just watching, but replying.

For two years, I woke up every day to hate mail and death threats. The only response Dr. Zoltan would offer was to correct their spelling and grammar.

It was bizarre to me that people took what was essentially a clown so seriously. I finally had enough of the negativity and deleted the videos.

An Idea is not a Plan. A Plan is not a Production.

What can we learn from this? Thousands of people hating me never did any harm to my Creative Career. If anything, it *helped!*

As an exercise, I recommend that you try it out. Create a Supervillain and send him out to stir up trouble. Under a pseudonym, get as many people to dislike you as possible. You'll get over your fear of rejection and criticism. After you get a hundred furious, poorly written emails, it won't matter anymore.

the seed

> *"The beginnings of great things cannot be seen by your naked eye."*
> — David Lee Roth, *Skyscraper*, 1988

Every creation needs a reason to exist. A conceptual point in space that it grows from. A central DNA that is present in every phase of its growth.

I call it **The Seed.**

Without it, your art will be in a state of Existential Crisis.

In screenwriting, there is a well-known conceptual hierarchy:

TITLE
LOG LINE
TREATMENT
SCREENPLAY

Each of these grows from The Seed and seduces you deeper into the work. (No, they're not *created* in this order, so stop freaking out.)

Title

This one is obvious. The title has to stand alone and speak for the movie in its absence. Think of it as an ambassador... or a traveling salesman. Often, it's all the audience has when making a decision, so make it a good one.

Log Line

This is where your tree grows a trunk. This is a short (often one-sentence) statement summarizing the movie. This is what you say when someone asks, "What's it about?" Keep it concise. Convey a vibe. Build tension into it, and whatever you do, don't resolve that tension. This is your opportunity to convey a Unique Identity for your movie. How is it different from everything else?

Treatment

There is a lot of debate over what exactly constitutes a Treatment, but I think of it as the branches of the tree. For the purpose of this concept, we'll agree that a Treatment is a one-page telling of the story, in everyday language. It might be broken up into three paragraphs, one for each Act of the story. Beginning-Middle-End. This is what someone reads when they want to know if you can tell a story.

Screenplay

These are all of the leaves and tiny branches. This is where all the detail goes. All the scenes, action, dialogue. For a feature film, it's 120 pages long. As a rule, no one wants to read it.

These are all further incarnations of The Seed. The central creative statement must be present in each of these forms.

Now let's apply this same principle to MUSIC.

Once upon a time there lived a virtuoso guitarist named Rongway Manglespleen.

Years ago, Rongway come up with a GREAT Seed — something that no one had ever thought of. He played classical music (like Bach and Paganini) on his electric rock guitar!

Whoa!

Instant hit.

He wrote a lot of music, and being a smart guy, he gave each piece a different Title. This helped his backup band tell the songs apart (some were in E Minor, some in B Minor).

His Treatments and Screenplays were dense, precise, and followed the industry-standard format.

Unfortunately, he only came up with *two* Log Lines in his entire career, and re-used one or the other on every song throughout his catalog of more than *thirty* albums.

They were:

1. Rongway Manglespleen shreds baroque scales and arpeggios over a minor-key chord progression on his electric guitar, in between vocal melodies sung by a vocalist with a wide vibrato.
2. Rongway Manglespleen shreds baroque scales and arpeggios over a minor-key chord progression on his electric guitar, minus the vocal interruptions.

(I know, they're technical-sounding Log Lines, but Rongway Manglespleen is a technical-sounding player. I had some fun with it.)

The point is, because he only had two Log Lines to choose from, all of his songs sounded *the same*. He may as well have written one long song. For 30 years, he told the same old recycled story, released the same product every year, and reached a limited audience of people who couldn't tell the difference.

What could poor Rongway have done differently?

First of all, he focused too much on his Screenplays. This is where a LOT of musicians get stuck, and I believe it is why the majority of movies and music are so boring. They flail away, showing off their mighty chops. *"Look at me go!"* But they tell no story, say nothing of importance.

All of those notes and words are just data. Decoration.

Ani DiFranco is an example of a musician who understands the importance of Log Lines.

She writes songs about a variety of subjects, plays them on a variety of instruments with a variety of moods, and, because of this, many of her songs are distinct and memorable. Her lyrics are so striking that I want to get tattoos of them.

AC/DC, in contrast, are another musical act (like Rongway) with only one Log Line. Luckily, it's a Log Line that their fans don't get tired of. As of 2010, *Back In Black* is the #2 top-selling album of all time. Forty-nine million copies sold.

You are your first audience.

Hey… do you wanna be rich or creative? (Shut up. Don't answer that.)

how to die a polymath

Everyone who wants a Creative Career should learn the basic mechanics and theory of:

- Writing
- Drawing
- Design
- Music
- Photography/Video

I don't mean you need to be good at all of them. Just get a grasp of the fundamentals. Crash course. The 101. Don't be afraid to jump in and learn, because you will use those skills for the rest of your life as a creator.

And if you're crazy (like I am), you'll be amazed at the concepts you can learn by making a lateral move from one form of expression to another.

Why?

Some creative concepts are best learned through looking, some listening, some through touching. If that weren't true, The Flying Spaghetti Monster would have given us some sort of electromagnetic pan-sensory organ that blends every perception into one. (Some call it a *brain*.)

If you're lucky, you'll experience a strange phenomenon called *Synesthesia*. Look it up.

Whatever you do, don't limit yourself. You've got five (sometimes six) senses. Use them to discover and make things. It's what you're here for.

Banish "most people are stupid" from your vocabulary. It's how most people get to be stupid.

section 3:
workspace

The magical workshop.
The secret factory.
The underground laboratory.

building your own spaceship

1 f you're going on this mission, you've got to build your spaceship. You're going to spend a lot of time in it. Seriously, like 20
or 30 years. Ten if you're *really* lucky.

That doesn't mean to run out to Target and buy a bunch of *deco-rations.*

Speaking of which, have you ever noticed that when people want
to change their lives, they think it means they need to go out and
buy things? Example: A girl who wants to start doing yoga will go
out and spend $300 on random junk — because she needs yoga
pants and yoga books and a yoga smoothie, right?

That's not what I'm talking about.

The first commandment in setting up a top-secret laboratory is
this:

You Must Take It Seriously.

I don't care if it's a broom closet — *Adult Swim* started in one.
Declare that what you are doing is *real* and *important.* Designate a
sacred room/desk/car/laptop/iPhone as The Spaceship. It's going to
be your helm. Your captain's chair.

Treat it with the utmost respect. Clean and organize it every day. It's a living shrine to your Creative Career.

Please do NOT put it in the same room as the dirty laundry, storage bins, and cat litter box. It's disrespectful. Your Creative Career must not be in exile. It must be the Central Command of your life. Everything else gets shoved away.

Here is what works for me:

I work out of what is usually called The Living Room of my apartment. Except it doesn't have the normal things a living room does. No couch, no civil war memorabilia, and, most importantly: no television.

For a workstation, I prefer a large flat surface. I have one of those folding banquet tables. It's cheap and is easy to move. It's seven or eight feet long. I can line up computers, hard drives, speakers, and whatever else I need to plug in.

I sit in a reclining office chair on wheels. It's great that it reclines and swivels, because that prevents me from sitting in one exact position for too long: I don't want repetitive stress injuries. I can rock back and forth, kick my feet up, and enjoy a robotic pair of arms that massage chakras in my back. (Just kidding, I'm not Tim Ferriss. Yet.)

Destructivity is the imagination gone wrong.

My studio isn't a place for people to hang out. I don't entertain guests. When clients come over, I've got a wooden stool, and that's all they get. Keeps them from getting comfortable and taking up my whole day with jiving and gossip. We're here to work!

I like to let the sunlight in. Every morning I open up the sliding glass door on the balcony and turn on all the lights.

There is a thick green tree directly outside my window. It keeps me from seeing my neighbors, who are probably as ugly as they are stupid. The early-morning sun pours directly onto my desk. (I find that sunlight has a major effect on my mood. During the year I lived in San Francisco, I got depressed from all of the gloom and fog.) Because of this, every day is spring cleaning for me. (**Most important advice in this entire book**: I don't allow visitors to wear shoes on my carpet. You'd be amazed at what a difference this makes. If you don't believe me, try it.)

You'll have to find out what works for you. And I'm going to repeat this throughout the book: "what works for you" means "what gets results." It doesn't mean "what caters to your bad habits." You might claim "It's organized chaos," or "I have a system to it."

Yeah, right.

tools & materials

Here is my philosophy on tools (guitars, computers, software).

They serve a *purpose*. The tools themselves are *not* the purpose.

People who buy expensive gear and don't use it are show-offs. They're not usually the people who get anything done.

It might make them feel good to have a pair of the latest and greatest Titanium Boxes Covered In Glowing Buttons, but what will it accomplish?

What are computers mostly used for? Resizing photos, typing text, and wasting time. Wow. The same thing we've been doing on them for ten years.

People argue about brands just like they argue about sports teams, political parties, and soft drinks.

It doesn't matter what brand anything is. A brand name is not a tool. It's a decal, a company logo, a self-referential advertisement for the non-entity who marketed it.

A tool is a transparent cable connecting Purpose to Results. If you even see the tool, you've missed the point.

> *"It's like a finger pointing away to the moon. Don't concentrate on the finger, or you will miss all the heavenly glory."*
> — Bruce Lee

Most of the great stuff throughout history was made with rudimentary tools, long before computers were invented. Tools are not a replacement for genius.

Eddie Van Halen changed rock music forever on The Frankenstrat — a $130 piece of junk guitar, painted with bicycle paint, wired wrong.

the hardware/software eternal chase

So you buy a new computer. Congratulations. It runs really fast, doesn't it?

Over time, you install new stuff. Updates. Patches. The latest OS. Better than the old one, right?

The result? Your computers run slow again. So you have to buy a new computer.

It's a trick.

Don't be in a hurry to upgrade your software.

the location: let's move!

Thinking of getting the heck out of that small town your parents picked for you? Maybe anywhere is better than where you are. But if you're going to do this right, take the following factors into consideration:

Population

How many people are trying to cram into one space, fighting for position at the traffic light, standing in line, pushing and shoving? That's no way to live. It's totally unnecessary. You need to conserve your energy. That means living in a place in which it is easy to do things. And by things, I mean uncreative, boring things: Going to the post office and bank, buying groceries, running errands. If it takes you all day just to go to the bank, you need to relocate.

Culture

What is the dominant culture? Is it full of poor people or rich people? What do most of the people do for recreation? Is it something healthy like hiking, or do the locals tend to get their exercise by carrying suitcases full of illegal pharmaceuticals? Is the dominant attitude one of upkeep, or do people just let things fall apart? Do they throw their garbage out in the yard, or do they have respect for the place they live in? I like to live in a place that is clean and full of productive people.

Find a mentor.

Safety

It's obvious that if you are sustaining physical damage from your surroundings, you should relocate. Still, I occasionally see some very unpleasant places that are densely populated. I don't want to fear for my life. I don't want to hear those police helicopters chasing someone running across my roof in the middle of the night. Unless you write crime novels, that's just not inspiring.

Infrastructure

By infrastructure, I mean how the city/town/village/your favorite moon base is designed. Does it make sense? Is it orderly? Was it planned, or did it just grow like an amoeba? More often than not, it's probably a huge mess. This goes hand-in-hand with Population. If the Infrastructure can't handle the Population, be prepared to sit in traffic for 4 hours a day, which is a part-time job you won't get paid for.

Weather

Is the weather hostile? Or is the outdoor environment comfortable year-round? How many months per year can you have your windows open? Are you affected by seasonal changes? I sure am. I like to have the windows wide open and let all of the sun in. I want to feel a cool breeze circulating through the house. I want to see trees and birds and mountains outside my window. In colder climates, people tend to not take care of themselves well.

Overall

In my experience, the most hassle-free, stimulating and creative places to live are college towns near major cities. The rent is typically very low to accommodate students, there is an atmosphere of learning and growth, the arts thrive, the public transportation is well developed, and it's generally very safe and clean. Many college towns are bicycle and pedestrian friendly. You most likely don't even need to own an automobile in these places. The low-budget student life is very similar to that of the stay-at-home Creative. And if you can get to a major metropolitan area in an hour or less, that's perfect.

When you are ready, try moving to New York City or Los Angeles (or some other "real" city) and be willing to go up against the most powerful and hard-working in the Creative Industry. You will discover the sheer magnitude of people (posers) trying to succeed, and learn which tired patterns they are stuck in. You will also learn that there are thousands of people with less talent than you, but who are willing to work 100x harder than you are. On the flip side, try living in the middle of nowhere and see what you can learn from that.

war story: the vacuum of venice, florida

I grew up in a small retirement town in Florida called Venice. (The 9/11 terrorists supposedly trained there, but that's another story for another book.)

Most businesses closed at 5 p.m., which meant there was nothing for young people to do. There was nowhere for bands to play, no comic book stores, no coffee shops to hang out in, and, of course, this was before the Internet existed. The nearest movie theater was 20 miles away in another city. If a teenager was out after dark, the police would shine a flashlight in his face and write up a report. Aside from wandering around in Wal-Mart or sitting in a Denny's, there was nothing.

It was hopeless. There was no escape. There was a saying that if you tried to leave, you'd just get sucked back in.

My friends and I grew up believing that we would never, ever, ever have a Creative Career.

Did that stop me from trying? No.

In 2001, a friend and I rented an office space. (Or should I say, "I pressured my friend into helping me rent an office space"?)

I wanted to do this for two reasons:

1. I thought that I could get my friend to take his drawing abilities more seriously if we actually had a dedicated creative space. I declared that *we would create a comic book!*

2. I needed to separate my own creative space from my mom's back porch. My desk/recording studio at the time was crammed in between cardboard boxes full of old clothes and a cat litter box.

We signed a lease on a nice second-floor, one-room office facing the middle bridge in Venice. I called it "The Tree House."

I established office hours. We got a phone, DSL, and an answering machine. We had three desks with computers and supplies. We even had a GWAR poster on the wall. A miniature couch-kind-of-thing for guests to sit on. It was "All-Time," as Eman Laerton says.

Always the delusional entrepreneur, I made up a company called 3-Legged Chair.

We printed up flyers for Web design service and distributed them all over town one night. We drove up and down US-41, sticking the flyers in the door of every business we could find. I was sure that if we covered the entire town, it was a perfect opportunity to start a Web design business. Most of Venice was not yet online, so this was perfect timing! As far as I could tell, no one else was trying to do it.

How many flyers did we put out? Hundreds.

How many calls did we get? None.

That was the end of 3-Legged Chair.

A week or two later, my friend stopped going to the office altogether. The comic book never got made.

After a couple of months, we packed it all up and moved out.

Until I was in my 30s, every "brilliant plan" I had for a Creative Career ended just like that one. Utter failure.

It never stopped me, and if I was lucky, I'd learn something each time. Things I wouldn't have learned if I hadn't tried and failed.

I'd drag people along, kicking and screaming (and sometimes biting) and it would result in nothing but wasted time and money. I even put that motto on my business cards: *"We DO Think It's Funny To Waste Time And Money!"*

Somehow I would always start again, thinking that "this time it will work." I was a frustrated pioneer trying to convince people to believe in whatever album, movie, company or website I was making.

Unfortunately, a Creative Career is something that the young people around me stopped believing in by the time they graduated from high school. I don't think anyone really bought into my crazy schemes, but they went along with them anyway... because there was nothing else to do!

That futility, however, was probably one of my greatest inspirations. It was like a threat. A dare.

My theory: "*Since I'm never going to amount to anything, what have I got to lose?*"

Venice, Florida, taught me how to work in a vacuum, with no reward.

The universe will pay you.

It's a skill, a thick skin I've developed that can get me through years of no payoff. There's no telling how long it might take to finish a creative project. It can be *years* of full-time work before you get a penny or a pat on the back — which is actually normal, except no one told me that back then!

But there's only so long you can survive in the desert, drinking your own urine.

Everyone has a breaking point. Mine was in mid-2006, at age 31. It hit me hard. I had been defeated. It was time to *flee.*

I moved to Los Angeles, and am now making tens of thousands of dollars a year from that same 3-Legged Chair business model.

Lesson: You can do everything right, but if you're in the wrong place, nothing will happen.

My advice: Get out of there.

the time is now

If you're mostly unencumbered and considering climbing into that escape pod, here are two things you must know:

1. There will never be a *right time.*

2. Don't plan it or talk about it, just *go.*

If you can do basic math, you can figure out how to survive.

health

Your health is your time is your energy is your life. Don't squander it. Taking responsibility for your Creative Career means taking responsibility for your avatar.

Don't kill it before you reach Level 80, you fool!

exercise

Use Your Body

Simply put, you have a body and you should use it. Don't live the life of a handicapped person.

When no one is telling you what to do, where to be, what to wear... it's too easy to let yourself go.

Try walking, jogging or biking. Get out and enjoy the daylight. It's something The Cubicle People never get to see.

Find something completely unrelated to your work. A hobby. Something that allows you to forget who you are. Something mindless and physical.

Yoga is a good example. It gets you back into your body. It requires so much focus and balance that you won't have time to worry about projects and deadlines.

> A technical person will always be subservient to an idea person.

diet

Premises for Food

Your body is an engine, food is fuel, and here are some principles for how they interact:

1. It is easier to consume calories than it is to burn calories.
2. You can easily consume a day's worth of calories in ten minutes.
3. What is sold as "food" is not always food.
4. In the old days, one day's worth of hunting would only provide one day's worth of food, so we had to start over every day.
5. Our bodies are not good at burning calories. However, our bodies are very good at storing calories.

It's no wonder one-third of Americans are obese. They're running a fat factory.

eat for your body, not your tongue

Chemists hired by Corporations have put chemicals in your food so that you won't want to stop eating it. It's You against Them.

With the emphasis on preservatives, stimulants and flavoring, we end up with "food" that has no nutritional value. Why? Because it's cheaper to put nutritionless crap in your body and make it taste good. They make more profit from filler and cardboard and sugar.

It would probably be healthier to eat the box it came in.

In nature, food that is good for you will tend to taste good in your mouth.

Unfortunately, we have amplified the flavor and removed all nutrition from most foods. Most of what people consider eating is merely passing large amounts of non-nutritious materials through their mouths and into their bodies.

Admit it if you are only seeking fame and fortune.

It is absurd that one small organ, the tongue, makes so many decisions for the body.

Here is a revolutionary idea I've mentioned before: Food is fuel.

Our bodies convert it into energy, and that energy is used to move your body around. If you don't move your body around, that energy turns into fat, and makes it even HARDER for you to move your body. That powerful energy from carbohydrates is almost always converted to fat if eaten at night (when you stop moving).

Never eat energy that you don't intend to immediately use.

Most Americans eat as if they're The Incredible Hulk, but their lifestyle is more like that of Professor Xavier. They end up looking like The Blob.

> Eat for your body, not for your tongue.

Skip the Middle Man

A lot of Americans are nothing more than an extension of their toilet. They take in food, chew it up, and 24 to 72 hours later, they feed it to the porcelain monster in the bathroom.

I say skip the Middle Man. Shove that handful of donuts straight into the toilet and flush 'em. Don't act as a living, breathing sugar filter for your toilet.

medicating

Recreational Drugs

Public Service Announcement:

> *Hi! I'm Carl King, and I have never used marijuana, tobacco, cocaine, LSD, heroin, crack, ecstasy, mushrooms, crystal meth, speed, PCP, or large amounts of cough syrup.*

I only consume small amounts of alcohol and caffeine under the following circumstances:

1. Red wine with dinner, but only when I am in the mood to be sleeping five minutes later.
2. Iced tea in the afternoon, but only if I have a lot of boring, repetitious work to do in my Creative Factory.

And that's all.

I have never seen proof of anyone who can habitually use recreational drugs for more than a few years without suffering consequences.

Sometimes it helps you to see things in a new way. But it's a dangerous shortcut.

I have seen too many brilliant, talented minds destroyed by drugs. It really does happen, and there is no glory in it. It rots your mind. It's simply sad that someone's ability to make great things goes away.

Pharmaceuticals

If you're going to take mass-manufactured chemicals to treat physical symptoms, be aware of this:

1. Pharmaceuticals are a profit-driven business.
2. The side-effects can be worse than the original problem.
3. Pills are not a substitute for lifestyle changes.

Investigate alternatives. Educate yourself. Don't just blindly swallow what they tell you to.

Find a Good Doctor

When selecting a humanoid with a stethoscope, take the following into consideration.

Your doctor should *listen* to you.

Your doctor should be *curious about your problems*.

Your doctor should address not only symptoms, but your *lifestyle*.

A doctor who walks into the room, sticks his finger up your butt, and then writes you a prescription, is a phony.

A doctor's office should be a place of holistic healing. It should not be a place of doom and gloom. You shouldn't be scared when you walk in. Are the administrative assistants smiling? Are there plants? Or is every possible surface of every object covered in ads for chemicals you can't pronounce?

Keep looking. Don't settle.

Extend Your Life

The result we're after with all of this talk of health and diet is *life extension*.

Spend the extra ten years writing that epic novel. Don't get old and sick until it's absolutely necessary. When you have finally developed enough wisdom and experience in your Creative Career, you'll wish you were younger so that you had the energy to enjoy it.

Your goal should be to stay healthy and young for as long as you can.

section 5:
learning

identify what you like and why

pick any band, maybe your favorite. Figure out what it is, that one thing that you could remove from their music that would destroy it entirely.

For instance, maybe Rage Against The Machine wouldn't work at all if they weren't presenting an anti-establishment image. It would just be a heavy funk/rap band.

What is central?

Your first clue is that it's usually the thing that anyone would remember after seeing them for ten seconds. That's usually "the gimmick" or "the hook." It's what you'd do if I asked you to imitate them right now.

Elvis? It's the voice, the hair, and that sneer. The jiggly legs. The jump suit. It's not the chord progression or song structure.

The rule is that it has to be easy to imitate or mock.

Richard Nixon: It's that "I'm not a crook" thing, or Watergate (but I think the quote is more memorable).

Abraham Lincoln: The beard and top hat.

Tony Robbins: The big teeth.

***Star Wars*:** The light sabers and Darth Vader voice. "I am your father." Totally overdone.

Read the owner's manual for your mind. Study logical fallacies, cognitive biases, and lateral thinking.

If people can't mock you or imitate you at a party, you're in trouble.

emulate others, but only as an exercise

Do not lose yourself in emulating others. This may happen a lot early on, while you are still learning and changing at an incredible rate.

Learn to take the ideas of others and embellish on them. What could be done with their ideas that they did not think of? Can you take their principles and apply them in a new way?

look again

Learn things, and then learn them again.

If you watch an interesting video that you learned something from, watch it again. Part of the time, you were probably integrating the information into your mind for the first time, and missing other important points.

Sometimes we have to learn the same lesson multiple times, but we understand it on a different level the next time around. Try to do some sort of review of ideas you have learned every day.

Sometimes ideas are forgotten after a short amount of time, and you need a reminder. Sometimes they make even more sense later.

Keep an Idea Journal. This book started as one.

see through the cheese

Some of the most fantastic musical ideas and performances are hidden behind the bad hairstyles, clothing and videos of '80s metal bands.

Few people know this, but the guys in Winger were all classically trained jazz-fusion and progressive-rock musicians. Look them up. Winger was only an entertainment project that they all contributed to for a few years.

Do your best to see through the cheese in life and recognize true talent and skill. There are important things to learn, and they are not always on display up front.

the spell is broken

> *"Don't part with your illusions. When they are gone you may still exist, but you have ceased to live."*
> — Mark Twain

When we first experience art, it's a mystery. A magic trick.

As creators, we gain knowledge of how things are made. We deconstruct. We look at the machine, the pixels, the dots on the page. We lose touch with that original mystery.

When we learn music theory, we're listening to the form, the sounds, the mechanics, instead of what is inside it. And what is inside it is not actually inside it — it is activated in us.

Art is self-activating software.

When they say that "art is in the eye of the beholder," it doesn't mean "everyone has a different opinion." It means our mind is the only place it can exist.

Not in the notes.

Not in the words.

Not in the brushstrokes.

When we listen to a record and hear the melody, we miss the point. Our own internal experience is what matters. Not the scales and time signatures.

A designer can obsess about typefaces, sizes, transparency, texture, color, margin, padding, kerning, italics, rotation, superimposing. But you're ignoring the meaning of the words you've typed.

Sculptures aren't made out of marble, they are made out of meaning.

Recipes are discovered. Not formulated. When we are in that analytical mindset, we are no longer creating. There's nothing there except the language of language. In other words, nothing.

If you take the robot apart and try to put it back together, it won't go.

mentors

Always seek out older, successful Creatives who believe in you.

A handful of people have changed my life, just by coming along and saying, "You're valuable." They didn't have to do that.

Mentor #1

In 4th grade, I somehow ended up in a gifted class, taught by Mentor #1. It was more like a psychological experiment. We ate popcorn with chopsticks, tended a garden, spoke in Japanese, played kickball, and went on a lot of field trips to a place called Pizza Peddler. Mentor #1 was the most inspiring schoolteacher I've ever had — I remember Creativity and Entrepreneurship being major topics. He openly detested the concept of Busy Work. His teaching methods were unusual and unpredictable, but he made me feel unique and talented. After being in his awesome class, I never liked school again. Nothing compared.

Mentor #2

I was 15, having a lot of problems: flunking out of school, no friends, never leaving my room. After discovering I could play guitar, my mom got me guitar lessons. She dropped me off at Troll Music every Saturday. The teachers didn't know what to do with me. I was introverted and refused to learn normal music, like blues or jazz. They gave me to Mentor #2, who spent the next couple of years, not teaching me guitar, but talking to me about Ayn Rand and Objectivism. He gave me a lot of confidence to break rules and use my own mind.

Mentor #3

When I was 17, Mentor #3 gave me a job stapling paper at his print shop. I was nearly a high school dropout. I had part of my head shaved and sported huge sideburns on the side of my face. I somehow convinced him to teach me typesetting and graphic design. I worked my way up and was awarded with my very own desk, which I treated like a factory. I loved that place so much that I skipped school every day to work there. He gave me my first opportunity to manage workflow, help customers, and be responsible for my work. He also taught me to drive.

Mentor #4

I was 21, still living with my mom, going to community college. I've only met Mentor #4 in person once, but I want to stress the importance of receiving acknowledgement and encouragement from someone successful. She is the manager of a famous rock star. She sent me an enthusiastic response to my demo tape way back then, and it changed my life. A kid in a small town getting a letter like that? Wow.

Mentor #5

When I was 24, I interviewed for a job at Mentor #5's small advertising agency, and instantly quadrupled my income. That same morning,

I had been sweating and running a paper-folding machine at another company (my desk was a cardboard box on the floor with my name on it). By the afternoon, I was wearing a tie and had two offices with three computers. I had never been given so much respect and responsibility by anyone. Mentor #5 would take me out on the weekends and we'd stay up all night listening to business motivational tapes. He believed I could do anything. Late one night, with tears in his eyes, he said, *"You're going to make it, Carl King."*

Mentor #6

I met Mentor #6 when I moved to San Francisco at age 26. He would pick me up and drive me around in his car, yelling at me. He is by far the most intelligent and talented person I have met. I had listened to his records and read about him in magazines since I was 16 years old, and here he was, acting like a big brother. The most important thing he taught me? There is much more to a creative person than the one thing they are known for.

Mentor #7

I was about to turn 31. I felt like giving up. I was back to living with my mom in Florida. For a few years, Mentor #7 had been a fan of my music. He could tell I was struggling, so he invited me out to California to hang out at Skywalker Ranch with him. After that, we went for some hikes around Lake Tahoe and he convinced me that I needed to move out to California. Best decision I have ever made. Changed my life.

I still keep in contact with as many of these people as I can, and ask their advice on major decisions.

If you are going to ask for career advice, ask someone who is qualified and experienced — someone who has been there and back.

Do not ask your depressed aunt, who has worked at a grocery store her entire life. Unless you want to work alongside her at the grocery store.

your heroes must become your peers

Being poor is expensive.

Realize that as you progress through your career, your heroes will become your peers. You may even find that you advance past them in certain areas.

Once you gain a lot of wisdom and experience, you may feel disappointment or resent them for seemingly letting you down. Your illusions may disintegrate.

Treat them (and everyone else) as you would a peer, and allow them to travel on their own path. Focus on your own goals rather than criticizing others.

Be your own hero.

traditional education isn't your thing?

Don't feel bad. I spent five years (that's right, five) in high school doodling, reading Ayn Rand books, and staring out of the library window. I never took it seriously, and I don't regret it.

My main objection was how much of my life was consumed by listening to teachers recite disconnected facts out of a book. (What happened to the concept of *concepts*?) I didn't identify with my classmates, got teased a lot, and just wanted to be at home practicing my guitar.

I would have never graduated from high school if I hadn't been placed in a "work at your own pace" program.

If you feel like you're too creative to stick with a traditional education, you're not alone.

More famous musicians, actors, directors, entertainers and comedians than you can imagine have opted to... ahem... *design their own educations.*

If you want to see the list, go to *carlkingcreative.com* and click on Resources.

Even ALBERT EINSTEIN (our society's model for Superior Intelligence) *dropped out of high school.*

Maybe he had better things to do?

should i go to that expensive music/ film technology school?

I get asked this question a lot.

Young people seem to want to go to That Expensive Music/Film Technology School because they can avoid entering the real world for another year or two. Or because their parents demand that they go to *some sort of college.*

As an alternative (I'm not saying to do this), maybe you could find other ways to spend that $50,000 a year?

For instance, move to Los Angeles and intern/slave/work as a personal assistant. That single year of fancy tuition could pay for three years of living and networking in Hollywood. Hit all of the movie, animation and recording studios.

You'll learn more doing that than any classroom or textbook will teach you.

the difference between a piece of paper and an education

A diploma is a certificate that proves the following:

1. You can read and write.
2. You can obey arbitrary rules.
3. You can memorize large amounts of data.
4. You have a high tolerance for other people's insanity.

That piece of paper tells the world:

"Hire me and I will fit nicely into your machine."

It says absolutely nothing about your creativity — which, in a Creative Career, is *everything*.

Of course, the world *needs* Cogs. We're all Cogs at one time or another.

The trick is to be a Cog in your own Creative Machine, instead of someone else's.

the five basic problems to solve

Speaking of learning, everyone should solve these basic problems before moving on:

1. Be clean.
2. Be on time.
3. Be organized.
4. Don't fight with people.
5. Don't spend more money than you earn.

Within the context of a Creative Career, success means "Exponential Return On Creative Investment."

Are you stuck? Are these incredible discoveries to you?

Sorry to be so harsh, but if you never get those figured out, you'll forever remain a child that is unable to deal with higher-level problems.

what is mastery?

We learn about ourselves and the world through our chosen art forms.

If he becomes a Master, a Writer will learn the same fundamental things about life that a Master Painter will learn.

It's not about the particular things we accomplish. Those are only the physical forms of the lessons. When you become a black belt, it's not about a belt itself or mastering some dance moves. You've demonstrated Mastery of the Self.

It just so happens that Self-Employment is a perfect vehicle for Self-Mastery.

the sign on your back

Ever notice that everyone you meet has something fundamentally wrong with them? Some important concept they don't grasp?

"He's such a talented guy. If only he would stop _____ or learn how to _____."

Learn to manage your own time.

Here's a theory: You have a tragic flaw, and only you are blind to it. To everyone else, it's blatant. Written loud and clear like a sign on your back. You can see the reaction to the sign in everyone's eyes, but no one will tell you what it says. In fact, they can't. If they did, you wouldn't hear the words. It's against the rules of the universe.

You can spend your whole life trying to read that stupid sign.

You may as well form a healthy working relationship with it, because it's not going away. No amount of introspection will directly reveal it. However, the more you address it, and the closer you can get to deducing what it says, the stronger art you will make.

Whatever it is on that sign, that's the good stuff.

section 6:
time
and
energy
control

walking the one true path

■ have this concept I call *The One True Path.*
1 Some of my friends believe it's an urban legend like the Loch Ness Monster, Bigfoot, or the U.S. Constitution.

What it means is this: everything in my life is unified toward my Creative Career.

And I've always believed that, unless I made it my highest priority, it would never happen. One after another, my Creative Career ideas would get interrupted, delayed or abandoned.

I needed to achieve something The Church of the SubGenius calls Time Control. Meaning…

I want to control all of my time.

In my experience, there is no "on the side."

If you must take side streets, make sure they point in the same direction as your One True Path.

the three shifts

A traditional day job ends up sucking away about 12 hours of your day. That is, if you include the time you spend getting ready, traveling to the office, eating lunch, traveling back home... and then that last unpaid hour you spend screaming about your boss.

Scientists have discovered the following facts:

1. There's not enough time in the day.

2. Things want to take up your time.

Pace yourself. To be able to balance everything, I break up my 12-hour self-employed workday into three shifts of four hours each. (This assumes you have achieved Time Control.)

Shift 1

9 a.m. - 1 p.m.

Inspiration

Any project that is long-term and requires creative vision I do first thing in the morning. It's when I get my best ideas. Writing this book is an example. Any project I am passionate about happens during this time. This shift is so important that

Wash your hair.

the other two shifts only exist to support it. The work done during this shift might not pay off for years, or even decades. My prime real estate is all about the future. I find that I'm not as creative later in the day, once I've come to my senses and started thinking analytically. There seems to be a correlation between being still half-asleep and being a genius.

Examples:
- Record an album of original music
- Write a philosophical essay or blog
- Create a cartoon series

Shift 2

1 p.m. - 5 p.m.

Technical & Freelance Work

This is where I pretend to be boring and do things for other people. I suspend my own identity and follow orders. I turn my creative skills into technical skills and sell them to support other artists and small businesses. This portion of my day is sacrificed to the God of Rent and Utilities. This is when I make sure my time-clock software is running. If we can't banish the monster, we can at least shrink it down to a manageable size.

Examples:
- Web design
- Video editing
- Wrangling work materials
- Emailing clients
- Sending invoices

Shift 3

5 p.m. - 9 p.m.

Research & Practice

I like to spend this time learning. I think of it as night school. It's usually free-form, but as I said before, this shift is directly in support of Shift 1. Everything I learn here gets used for whatever long-term creative project I'm immediately obsessed with.

Examples:
- Watch a movie and analyze its structure.
- Practice drawing.
- Walk to the bookstore and read trade magazines.
- Listen to podcasts/interviews.

The problem is that when I work on a routine/schedule every day, I get bored, anxious, and uninspired.

Recommendation: Spend your best creative energy on your own projects, first thing in the morning. Without these long-term creative projects, your life is ultimately going to be in someone else's hands.

day on/day off

You can also try working one day for Them, one day for You, back and forth. You might need to squash and squeeze those shifts, or even combine them.

Whatever you do, take control and find balance. Don't live a scattered life, only reacting to whims and distractions.

to-do lists

When you're an employee, you have a To-Do List. The boss sends you an email, and it goes on the list. You don't question it, you just do it.

Beware. It's easy to fall into this same trap when you're self-employed.

You're so used to blindly taking care of tasks and errands that you never learn to say no — not even to yourself!

In a day job, you're a productivity machine, making sure that list gets smaller each day. That's all that matters.

Until now.

When you're self-employed, you have the power. You can look at your To-Do List and select which items will achieve outcomes. Believe it or not, all items are not of equal importance. You can prioritize and even delete stuff without first doing it.

How awesome is that?

Remember, clients are not your "boss." You can actually tell them you are not going to do their work. (In a nice way, I hope.)

How does THAT feel? At first, it's strange. Scary. Liberating.

You've been trained all your life that you'll be fired if you say No. Don't worry. Self-Employed is a perpetual and enlightened state of Fired.

One last thing to be aware of: **Compound Procrastination.**

If you're not careful, you'll end up with too many unrelated things on your To-Do List… scattered errands that make no sense when viewed as a workflow. Since there's no possibility of arranging them in any linear order, you can't get started.

Defeat!

Sometimes the only answer is to set aside the factory mindset and start on one of them. You'll be surprised at how fast it will all be over.

efficiency!

Some activities are more enjoyable when you take your time.

Work is not one of them.

I strive for efficiency in all things. I don't want to double back, carry things I don't need, pay extra fees, make another phone call, sit in traffic, stand in line, or talk to anyone I don't have to talk to.

These are things that contribute absolutely nothing to my life.

If you have a long project ahead of you, invest a small amount of time up front on Workflow Design. Can you change the order of or combine two steps? If you analyze your workflow, can you save a lot of time and energy? The answer is always yes.

Don't do stuff the long way.

If work, in and of itself, were a good thing, we wouldn't have invented simple tools, like wheels and baseball bats and toilet paper.

free time

A lot of artists value free time more than anything. I can relate.

In my 20s I worked as a temp at a real estate office. More specifically, I sat in an upper-class model home all day, alone, daydreaming, listening to classical music on the intercoms.

Lift weights with your mind.

No Internet. No cell phone. Expensive furniture to lounge around on. It was like being rich. It was paradise.

One day, the real estate agents figured out that they could give me all their busy work.

We all know that photocopying stacks of documents is not how a creative person should spend his time.

The machine I used was old-fashioned and deserved to be taken into a field by the guys in *Office Space*. Those glorious eight-hour days I spent staring out the window were to be spent on paper jams? No.

Brilliant idea: At lunchtime, I took all the documents to a copy store and paid to have them done, out of my own pocket. My boss never knew, and was stunned by my speed. It probably consumed my whole paycheck every week, but who cares? I lived at home and could get away with it.

Sometimes free time is priceless.

ideas, plans & productions

Don't confuse yourself.

Ideas, Plans and Productions are all different things.

Idea

I want to produce a comic strip. That would be cool.

Plan

I will write and draw a weekly comic strip. It will be called ____, starring three characters named ____, ____, and ____. It will cost me ____ for materials, and I will publish it on ____ dot com. It will be black & white. My intended audience: ____.

Production

I've released six episodes of the comic strip, written premises for an additional ten, and am receiving criticism, both positive and negative. I'm fine-tuning it and developing the characters — getting lots of ideas about their distinct personas as time goes on. Fans are emailing me and also quoting the characters on their Facebook pages.

Lesson: Some Ideas don't deserve to be turned into Plans. That's OK. Ideas can show up somewhere else and get used later. Enjoy them for what they are, and then go ahead and start on new Ideas and Plans.

Too often, people come up with a great Idea and Plan, then get discouraged because the Production doesn't happen. It feels like a failure, but don't worry about that. At least you're doing something.

Betray the tribe.

If you keep going, doing this over and over, you'll get better at knowing which Ideas will ultimately deserve a Plan and Production.

The fact is, only a small number of Productions succeed.

But don't worry. Ideas are everywhere. They are the dirt you have to dig in. There is no shortage of dirt, and no shortage of Ideas. What matters is that you keep digging.

Don't freak out. It will never be possible to execute every single Idea there is.

"Never underestimate the power of an idea."
— Old Friend

Chances are, someone else has the same idea that you have. But are they going to do anything with it? Probably not. It's hard work to Plan and Produce.

That was the difference between Ween and zillions of stoner kids with 4-tracks.

EROEI: the vengeful god at the center of the galaxy

EROEI is a vengeful god who lives at the center of the galaxy. As punishment for wasting the energy of other gods, he was imprisoned in a hyper-dimensional wormhole 13.75 ±0.17 billion years ago.

From there, he punishes the human race. Primitive civilizations know him as the immortal enemy of efficiency, practicality and profit. Some of his most notable contributions to planet earth are tax forms, speed bumps, and the DMV.

And now he has cursed you.

Just kidding.

EROEI stands for *Energy Returned On Energy Invested*.

Realize this: From the day you're born, you leak energy. It's a slow drain. *You don't get it back.*

What you do with the rest of it, until it's all gone, is up to you.

I recommend investing energy instead of spending it.

Don't just watch movies. *Act* in them.

Don't just read books. *Write* them.

Don't just listen to music. *Play* it.

Each of these experiences is active and has an *exponential reward*.

Focus the majority of your time and energy on activities that are consequential to your future. Don't just throw your time and energy into a black hole.

Or EROEI will have won.

Some activities are more enjoyable when you take your time. Work is not one of them.

section 7:
money/ finances

my ideas on money won't make you rich. Sorry!

What they will do is protect your sanity while on this adventure.

If you want to get rich quick, maybe you should try a different career, like running an oil company (or rebuilding stuff that the oil companies blew up).

you don't want to be rich

Rich people are stupid. They spend their money on things that don't make any sense. They've lost their perspective on the creative energy in the universe.

Think of how many incredible albums could be made instead of buying that fancy couch.

You don't want to be rich, you want to be responsible for large amounts of money (energy).

There's a difference.

Even though rich people think they do, no one owns money or energy. Certain people are merely able to temporarily re-direct it from one place to another. Think of these people as points of intersection, where lots of money passes through.

It's ok to be The One.

78

They can direct it wisely or unwisely, apply it to something useful or useless. But either way, it will keep moving, and eventually wander away if they are foolish.

lemonade-stand capitalism

Practice "Lemonade-Stand Capitalism."

Is money a good thing? Yes.

But money is not really *The Bottom Line*.

What matters is the effect we create with that money. The outcome. The end result.

Money is a generic tool that can be used to do good or bad things. You must be responsible, conscious, and make wise choices not only with how you spend it, but with how you *acquire it*.

If you run a lemonade stand, keep it to a scale where the greatest number of people involved *still care about the lemonade*.

The further you get away from that boutique, do-it-yourself model, the worse things usually get. You'll end up with lemonade without real lemons, pumped full of fake flavors made in a shadowy laboratory, and an army of vacant retail soldiers in poofy yellow hats.

You don't want to become a faceless corporate machine that inefficiently squanders long-term resources for the sole purpose of making executives wealthy in the short term.

Don't just make a number on a spreadsheet bigger. That's where things go wrong. Always remember what that number represents.

Run the best little lemonade stand on Earth.

eternal vigilance: financial accounting software

If you're committed to not being homeless, go out and buy yourself accounting software.

I have used QuickBooks (*intuit.com*) for five years. It's one of the most important pieces of software I own.

Why?

1. When I'm being paid by ten different people, I need to know how much money I have right now, and how much I will have (projecting a month or more in advance).
2. I track all of my monthly expenses (food, rent, utilities) to make sure I'm not spending too much.

3. I analyze which of my products and creative services are generating the most profit. Which clients are the best investment of my energy?

4. It syncs with my bank accounts.

"Independence requires eternal vigilance."
— Benjamin Franklin

the universe will pay you

Every artist starts out with the fear that he will never make a living.

Don't worry. If you do great work and share your creative value with the universe, it will get around to paying you.

Just know it might take a long time, especially for your own creative projects.

Refuse to accept your current situation.

In *Outliers*, Malcolm Gladwell talks about the "10,000-Hour Rule," which states that it takes 10,000 hours of practice to become an expert at something. That translates to part-time for 10 years or full-time for 5 years.

I don't think that number is always a steady accumulation of experience and knowledge. I believe it's more like the average amount of time it takes you to:

1. Give up for good, or

2. Figure out one good trick to make money off your weird stuff.

Nothing makes you an "expert" on a subject more than being able to do it for a living.

So, for the first 10 years (or 10,000 hours — whichever comes first), consider the universe one big client with a lazy accounting department.

Until then, you will get paid for your creative work, in varying amounts, through multiple sources, at unexpected times.

You asked for it.

not everything should be measured numerically

With the importance of measurement in our society, we've become fixated on the arbitrary numbers in time clocks, speed limits, and bank accounts.

But some things don't need to be measured numerically.

Money is only one way of transferring energy/value between one person and another. Like any rule or law, it shouldn't be relied upon beyond its application to real life.

Don't get locked into only one economic system. Not everything can be measured in dollars, euros, pesos, or whatever type of colorful paper or metal you and billions of your friends are hypnotized by.

Money is abstract and subjective, not a fixed material value. Why on earth should things like Health and Art be channeled through this bizarre means of measuring?

losing the game isn't more noble

If life is a big game of Monopoly, what's wrong with winning? Why is losing more noble? If someone will always lose, why does it have to be you?

keeping your balance

As a practical matter, I can't stress **Cashflow** enough.

"Cashflow" can mean different things. In this case, I'm referring to a *steady flow of payments received.*

Paying yourself requires measured discipline and vigilance.

When you're not receiving a steady paycheck from a company, it helps to create the illusion of steady income.

Example: If you make $50K a year, try to receive $1,000 a week. Keep it steady. I don't like to get paid by five people all at once.

Figure out your Cashflow for an entire month ahead of time. The problem with this is that a lot of people are freaked out by how dry and predictable it is. It's as if they're afraid to look at the future and how it will probably work out. They'd prefer to believe that something magical and unpredictable will happen.

But that's OK — unpredictable things will happen, and not always in your favor. The more you plan out your month, the better the chances are that you won't be destabilized by surprises.

the problem with materialism

Materialists, listen up, because I have another Helpful Delusion for you:

All that stuff you've stacked up — the DVDs, comic books, statues, clothes, posters, boxes full of photos, random crap crammed into the extra rooms you built onto your house... you're wasting your energy, because it's not actually *yours*.

You can't truly own anything in this world. You can only borrow it/rent it until you die.

I avoid all "Kipple," a term coined by Philip K. Dick:

> *"Kipple is useless objects, like junk mail or match folders after you use the last match or gum wrappers of yesterday's homeopape. When nobody's around, Kipple reproduces itself. For instance, if you go to bed leaving any Kipple around your apartment, when you wake up the next morning there's twice as much of it. It always gets more and more."*

Get rid of stuff if you don't use it. Most of what you own is mass-produced junk that can be easily acquired again if you need it for something.

As Tyler Durden said, "The things you own, end up owning you." (*Fight Club*, Chuck Palahniuk)

If you don't get rid of it now, you'll find yourself carrying boxes of it up and down stairs in a few years, wondering where it all came from.

lose everything

You need to be willing to scrap it all and start over.

If you don't stay in a state of re-invention in real-time, life will come along and kick your ass when you least expect it. You'll lose that "secure" job, your wife will cheat on you, and things will fall apart.

Be OK with that.

You might need to lose everything and start over many times. Destruction is part of Creation.

As one of my mentors used to say, "Once you hit bottom a couple of times, it won't scare you anymore."

being poor is expensive

As if being broke isn't bad enough, banks (and the rest of the business world) love to punish us for being poor.

It's exponential.

If you operate near zero, you'll find that you are paying all sorts of extra charges: overdraft fees, finance charges, late fees, check-cashing fees, and bizarre penalties that a financially stable person doesn't have to pay.

The good news is that if you can learn some self-discipline with your money, you won't experience them anymore. Stay as far away from $0 as you can.

ALWAYS plan ahead and build a buffer for yourself, to avoid getting sucked into the Money Black Hole. You'll find that, ironically, an abundant lifestyle is less expensive and requires less energy than being poor.

live in the future

Plan things a day in advance, then plan things a week in advance, then a month in advance, and so on. Learn to live in the future.

Prepare for your life, rather than always living in a state of panic and emergency. You will be amazed at how much energy and time this frees up to be creative.

patching the holes

In the same way that we're all leaking energy, we're also leaking money.

When you're a Creative Career Soldier, every dollar you spend is another dollar you will have to work for.

Food

There is no reason you should be spending more than $5 a day on food. That's only $1,825 a year. Restaurants are not places to get food. Restaurants are places to sit in and be entertained by waitresses. I've got this friend who paid $6,152 to eat in 2009. If someone had said, "I'll pay you an extra $4,327 cash if you can live on $5 a day," that would have saved me (I mean him) 100 hours of freelancing.

> You do not need permission to be creative.

Clothing

Don't buy those expensive skate-shop T-shirts with logos splattered all over them. You're just paying 4x extra to advertise a logo for a company who doesn't do anything except print logos on T-shirts.

They'll wear out fast, so don't fall into the trap. Buy blank shirts from Target or Goodwill. I buy about three new blank t-shirts per year, usually for my birthday.

Magazines

Don't buy magazines in a store. Subscribe. Better yet, read them online.

Avoid Retail

To explore, you first have to be lost.

Try to buy directly from manufacturers and distributors. Whenever there is a storefront involved, there's always a markup to pay for electricity, sales associates, window cleaning, etc.

Buy In Bulk

Whenever you can, buy in bulk. Toilet paper, staples, socks. If it's something you'll use every day for the rest of your life, buy as much of it as you can at once. Take advantage of quantity discounts.

buy money, don't save it

When you put money into a saving's account, what you are essentially doing is buying money.

Perhaps this is why Benjamin Franklin said:

"A penny saved is a penny earned."

Why don't more people do it?

Because it's boring!

Yet it's probably one of the smartest things you can buy, right up there with education and experience.

Don't try the old excuse that you "don't make enough money to save." If you can afford to buy cigarettes, beer and cable television, you can afford to buy money.

If everyone wants money so badly, why are they in such a hurry to spend it?

Go out and buy some money right now. Even if it's only $5.

consider yourself lucky...

...if you make *any money at all* from doing something creative. Many great artists, poets and inventors die bankrupt and insane.

section 8:
the
business
side of the
business

hobbyists, amateurs & professionals

a Pro is someone who won't come out on stage and do a drum clinic in a jazz bar until everyone extinguishes their cigarettes. A Pro asks people dining on the other side of the room to stop talking while others are trying to learn. An Amateur does not believe he deserves to teach anyone anything, much less tell anyone what to do.

Before releasing a live DVD of his rock concert, a Pro learns how to edit all of the footage himself in Final Cut Pro. An Amateur gives up or hires someone else to do it wrong because he is "only good at playing guitar."

A Pro learns every aspect of recording and releasing his own record (including studio construction, soundproofing, artwork, manufacturing, distribution, advertising) and makes millions of dollars off his homemade recording. An Amateur waits for someone else to succeed for him.

A Pro gets one break in his early 20s and goes on to exponentially turn it into a lifelong career... leading bands, touring the world, and releasing new rock albums into his late 40s. An Amateur self-sabotages, complains, and moves back to Ohio after a few bad auditions.

Alienation is good. Artists spend a lot of time alone.

A Pro studies peripheral topics related to his primary field of expertise — such as how to maintain his instrument and equipment. An Amateur is at the mercy of unknown technology that is never set up right.

A Pro studies EQ and learns to name specific frequencies of feedback by ear, even though he is a drummer. He gets so good at it that he does his own drum mix in concert, while playing. An Amateur is afraid of metronomes.

A Pro goes for it, whether that means moving to Los Angeles or creating an Internet cartoon in his living room with his brother. An Amateur doesn't think he is ready for either one.

A Pro studies his craft relentlessly. An Amateur studies losers relentlessly, and eventually becomes one.

So what about Hobbyists? Hobbyists love to do what they do, but they don't really take it seriously. There's no pressure for these guys. They have fun on the weekends with it, and it is nothing but a positive experience. Nothing wrong with that.

On the other extreme, a Pro is a world-class athlete who trains every day... adjusting his time, social environment, finances, diet and mental attitude in order to be the best at what he does. For him, it is also nothing but a positive experience. The work is a massive reward in itself.

With all of these things in mind, we soon discover that an Amateur is really just a deluded Hobbyist who masquerades as a Pro — by mistakenly expecting to support himself off his Hobby. Hobbyists don't like to work. They just like to have fun.

And it's the same with Amateurs.

So if you don't choose to be a Pro, consider just being a Hobbyist. Whatever you do, don't be an Amateur.

got factory?

If you need to hire someone, shop for a Pro with a fully armed and operational creative battle-station. If you don't see a factory, don't trust him. Just assume the work will never get done. You want someone who is ready to put your project onto the assembly line, because that's what he does every day, for a living. Don't hire a Hobbyist (see below).

When I was shopping for an artist to illustrate the character bible for my animated TV show concept, *The Mysterious Octopus*, I went with Lance Myers. Why?

1. He has an impressive resume (animator for BioWare, lead animator of *A Scanner Darkly*).
2. He produces his own Internet cartoons that show he is a master of writing, storytelling, and strange comedy.
3. His line art is crisp and he expresses dramatic ideas through color and lighting.
4. He lives in Texas, which means he probably has a real life, family, and friends outside of the hustle.

Yes, those were my reasons. Most importantly, I knew that if I paid him and gave him a deadline, he'd crank out the work. Was all of it 100% what I envisioned? No. But it was AWESOME. At that high level of creativity and productivity, the only disagreements are over specific details — not over quality. It's more like, "Which color Lamborghini do you want?"

Beware of working with people who don't have a factory. You need to be able to drop projects into the assembly line.

"If you want something done, give it to a busy person."

It takes a lot of work for someone just to get the factory up and running. It's dangerous to hire someone who doesn't do it full-time.

the eternal audition

Be prepared to spend your entire life trying to prove yourself. A Creative Career is the only job in the world where you might never actually get hired.

Sacrifice is
not failure.

marketing/ communication

sales is not a bad word

helpful Delusion: When you see the words "sales" or "marketing," replace them with "communication."

Artists are notoriously bad salesmen. Their catchphrase is, "I hate selling myself."

That's because their first instinct when trying to sell themselves is to imitate a bad salesman. They've learned from amateurs. Everything they know about sales, they've experienced through telemarketers, ticket scalpers, door-to-door solicitors, used car commercials, those subscription cards that fall out of magazines, and homeless beggars.

Sales is not about beating people up until they buy.

Sales is about connecting with people. Tell a story they can relate to. The best salesmen are not salesmen. They're friends. You never see them coming, because they're not. They're so likable and trustable and human that you assume they're off-duty.

The truth is, those are the ninjas who make the most sales.

Brute force is for salesmen who are scared to get real. They feel guilty and manipulative. In that case, they *are* being manipulative, because they don't really care about the people they're talking to. They care about selling Widgets.

Widgets are any generic product divorced from personal meaning (story). Selling one Widget is no different from selling another. Just look at the Home Shopping Network. They've got a different product every five minutes. No one can honestly believe in selling that stuff. There's no story or significance beyond the commission.

You are never too old. A Creative Career is a lifelong commitment.

If you're selling Widgets, you're dead.

Don't sell the container. Sell the content (the meaningful story), and people will buy the container. "My new book is now available on Amazon" is as unimaginative as saying "The dimensions of my book are 6x9, it's 225 pages, and contains 50,000 words."

Is it really about that? That's the message you're here to share with the world? That's what you think people are interested in?

Be a great storyteller, connect with people, and you will sell more Widgets than you can imagine.

story trumps all

Want to be a musician?

It doesn't matter if you can't sing.

It doesn't matter if you only have one microphone.

It doesn't matter if your guitar is missing strings.

It doesn't matter if you don't know what a verse or chorus is.

If you can tell a powerful story with your music, that's all that counts.

It's the same with art, writing, film, and any other strange way of expressing yourself that you can invent.

Always try to connect with some fundamental idea that you want to share with the world. Make sure there's something behind what you do.

Music is not the notes, technique, or theory. Music is meaning.

I wasn't there, but I am pretty sure that when Black Sabbath wrote the song "Iron Man," they weren't thinking of beats per minute, scales, and voice leading. Chances are, they were thinking angry, scary, evil. The music they played is nothing but a collection of symbols to convey that.

Don't get stuck in the symbols. Don't tell the story of when Mixolydian met 7/8. Don't get stuck in the Language of Language.

throw away your tools

You can officially forget about quality, technique, tools and form. A great story can be told regardless of those limitations. Even if all you can do is talk, you can find a way to tell a powerful story.

When are you ready to be a successful storyteller? When you're ready to tell the world about itself.

the worship of technique

Bad writers, bad musicians, bad artists, bad actors, and bad people in general focus on technique above all else.

Why?

When we start out in the arts, technique is our primary obstacle. It takes years of practice to build chops. Later on, it's hard to let go of that enemy. We still want to prove ourselves and show off.

Don't show off with technique. Show off with great ideas.

Words like "plethora" and "*per se*" and zillions of words ending in "ly" don't tell a story. They just rattle around and make noise. You could show off and write "He filled the bucket 14484/28968ths," or you can just write "He filled the bucket halfway" and get on with it.

Get the writing out of the way of the story. Get the playing out of the way of the music. Get the special effects out of the way of the movie.

You've got to tell a story — a *narrative* — and it needs to be grounded. Primal. Simple.

It's not because the majority of people are cavemen. It's because a caveman exists in each of us. And "if the caveman ain't happy, ain't nobody happy."

The greatest art can be reduced to a simple, central premise (a High Concept) that anyone can understand. The rest is decoration.

text & subtext

In communicating, as in screenwriting, pay attention to what should be put into text and what should be subtext.

Text is what you say. Subtext is what you mean.

Sure, it's an elementary concept, especially to screenwriters. Bury the exposition. Don't "talk the plot." Right?

Then why not apply those same rules to marketing/sales?

If you go around talking about how important and famous you are, the subtext is going to give you away. If you're really that important and famous, you wouldn't go around saying it. You'd be over it. (If you think the dialogue in Hollywood movies is bad, you should eavesdrop on wannabe actors.)

Tip: How to find the most important and successful person at any Hollywood party — it's the guy who isn't talking. He doesn't have to. He's not the one with the business cards, aviator sunglasses, faux-hawk and sport coat, wheeling and dealing and shaking hands. He doesn't have to make anyone like him.

Don't try to shoehorn every single interaction into a marketing pitch. It's often better to convey meaning without words. Pay attention to that when conducting your business.

honking

I see a lot of what I call "Honking" on Social Networking sites like Facebook and Twitter.

A "Honker" is an unimaginative artist whose sole purpose for Social Networking is to promote their latest CD, book, movie, or live performance — "honking" obnoxiously like an ugly, fat goose rather than "tweeting" like a pretty little bird. These perpetrators should be responded to by civilized users with a simple "Honk!"

It looks like this:

> *"Hey everybody, check out my MySpace page. The first 20 people to download my new free commercial get a 13.5% discount on my latest flier."*

or...

> *"We have T-shirts and stickers, please vote for my new record, I will be playing live at 8pm, 2-for-1 drinks if you print this page, come and check us out!"*

or...

> *"My new book,* How To Sell Books On The Internet, *is in the Top 20 on* InternetMarketingBlogReaders.com. *Order 3 copies and get a free 2-month subscription to my* Selling StuffBigMoneyMarketing *RSS Feed!"*

Impersonal, generic messages full of data that don't amount to much more than "Click On My Link" and "Buy My Widget" don't work. (Not if you're trying to build an authentic career, anyway.)

Here is what Frank Zappa said about this in an old interview:

> *"I make the act of doing business part of the creative act. I involve it in the overall concept of what I do. Which has led to some rather amusing album covers, I think, and some pretty bizarre advertising campaigns for the products. If you have to advertise, make it interesting. If you have to do an album cover, make it interesting. If you have to do an interview, make it interesting. You should always make it interesting."*

In other words, if you're advertising something creative, why not advertise it creatively? Why does the creativity have to *stop?*

Frank Zappa wasn't just selling albums. He was *sharing his imagination with the world.* And he applied his imagination to everything he did. His interviews, which he did for free, are priceless. His "product" was not just his music. The guy was oozing with creativity, and nothing could be within five feet of him without getting sucked up into it. It just so happened that a portion of that ended up on records. How could it *not?*

It is my belief that in a Creative Career, product-based selling is worthless. We have to evolve beyond "product-centric" thinking. In this new world of copy-everything-with-one-click, revenue has to come from:

Walk the One True Path.

1. Live, Personal Interaction. You can't copy this. Musicians, think Live Shows. Authors, think Workshops. Philosophers, think Retreats. It's life-changing to be there in a room with a real human being who isn't scripted and edited. Ask any question you want! Steve Vai, a famous rock guitarist, recently put on a Master Class. He charged $325 per student, limited to 70 spots. Can you say, "$22,750 in 3 hours?" Show up with your guitar and amp, talk for a few hours. "No band? No band problems." Incredible! Why aren't more semi-famous musicians doing this?

2. Limited Edition, One-of-a-Kind Collectibles. Forget trying to sell things that people can download. Take a cue from the comic book/sci-fi audience (which is becoming monstrous, if you haven't noticed) and sell statues, mugs, anything that someone can put on their desk, hold in their hand, touch. Nothing that is mass-produced. Make it special, make it rare. Make it cool. I know a guy who collects original pencil & ink drawings from comic books. What does he fantasize about if he had millions of dollars? "Dude, I would buy so many original Conan Pages." These things can sell for thousands of dollars. If you're an artist, why aren't you doing this?

Everything else that can be downloaded is Free. Music, PDFs, Blogs, Images. Give it away. This is a new world and that's the way it works. Don't try to go into business selling something that everyone already gets for free.

That's called a *Bad Business Idea*. Like selling snow to Eskimos.

It might last a little while (some people are still buying CDs for some reason), but you're doomed if you don't figure this one out. Supply and Demand, remember? HONK!

naming your company

The best names for creative companies are:

1. Creative and fun — the subtext being: The person who made it up is also creative and fun.
2. Easy to spell, easy to remember. "What was the name of that company?"
3. Unusual. Things that are different are memorable. Check out the concept behind Seth Godin's *Purple Cow*. (That's another easy-to-remember name, yes?)

I love these names:

Titmouse (animation company behind *Adult Swim* cartoons)
Industrial Light & Magic (visual effects company behind *Star Wars*)
Bad Robot (J.J. Abrams' production company)

One of my first companies was called Ed Furniture. My mom was right. It was a terrible name for a record label.

Don't overthink it.

The production company behind *Adult Swim* is called Williams Street. Why? Because their building is on Williams Street in Atlanta. Duh. But, somehow, that creepy logo at the end of their cartoons works on me every time.

If what you do is fantastic, the name is secondary.

I think *Star Wars* is an awful name. We've seen it so many times that we've gotten used to it. A lot of the names in that universe are complete gibberish, yet they've come to be powerful symbols for us.

Chewbacca? Come on.

the downward spiral

We've all heard or said the phrase *"Most people are stupid."*

Banish it from your vocabulary.

We've created a downward spiral known as Popular Media.

If we assume most people are stupid, we make stupid art. Kids grow up and see that art, and they become stupid. They go on to make stupid art, and they complain: *"Most people are stupid."*

I notice that the people who say this phrase all the time are the ones who make the stupid art in the first place. I think it's an excuse to make stupid art and sell a lot of it.

Maybe most people aren't stupid, and it's just a mutual illusion.

Either way, don't contribute to the downward spiral.

Don't be stupid.

web design for artists

I've designed about 50 artist websites.

What I've learned is this:

There are no websites, only content.

If you're on your way up in the business, get the website out of the way and get to your message. Don't bury your most important content three levels deep. If you're a photographer, director, or musician... put the best stuff on the front page.

Fact: The average visitor looks at your site for 30 seconds. If you don't believe me, look at your stats.

Despite what consultants tell you, there's not one magical way to design a website. The design trends change every few months. Most of it is jargon (similar to the nonsense a New Age Lifestyle Coach makes up) that does nothing but put money into the Web designer's pocket.

As an artist, your only trick is: Have kick-ass content.

Unless you've got that, no one cares about buttons or bouncy things. No one is going to read all of your fabulous text. No one will

"Enter Email Address To Subscribe" or "Add To Cart" or "Follow Me On Whoopdeedoo."

Website visitors are distracted, impatient, and in a hurry. Their friends are instant messaging them, they're hoping the boss doesn't walk in, and they're only at your site while a video of a baby is downloading.

So keep it simple.

1. Home page with your main point that can be digested in thirty seconds. One title, one photo, one media clip, and one descriptive paragraph.

2. All the rest of your junk (press clippings, links to other links, behind-the-making-of-the-making-of-the-video videos) goes in the basement of the website, for those random stalkers who actually care about the excruciating mechanical details of your creative labyrinth.

Emulate others, but only as an exercise.

show me the panda

What is the result you want out of your website?

In other words, what action do you want the visitor to take?

Examples:

• Buy a panda.
• Laugh at the pictures of pandas.
• Subscribe to your podcast about pandas.

Those are specific actions. Get it?

Now clear a short, straight path to the panda button, so they can push it.

Center aisle. Big display. Spotlight.

Get everything else out of the way. No distractions. No clutter.

Hide the 71% non-panda stuff that isn't getting the results you want.

When you're on your way up, you can't afford to build anticipation. Just show me the panda, already.

pleasing the demigods of professionalism

I notice this: Too many people have the wacky idea in their minds that they need to be "professional." I say they've got to be the victims of mind control or brainwashing.

Keep this on the "downlow," but there are rumors about a hypothetical group of people... more like a secret society called The Demigods Of Professionalism.

All we know is that these people are incredibly judgmental and will take jobs and opportunities away from the artist who does anything remotely edgy or weird.

I'm not entirely convinced I've met one of them, but I've felt their presence.

This I know for certain: They have Secret Passwords. One of them is "Utilize." Every time I hear someone say that word in the place of "Use," I have to wonder if they've been to that Secret Place where the Demigods of Professionalism meet on Tuesday nights and type resumes.

professional does not mean formal and corporate

Professional does not mean Formal and Corporate. All it really means is that you are for real. It means you really do work in the business you claim to, and that you're solid and reliable.

Professional is often subtext. You demonstrate that you are professional. You don't say you're professional with fancy words. It's something that people have to see to believe.

Don't be afraid to be your unique self. In this world, you can't afford to be any more boring than you already are. Every important and famous person I have ever met has a sense of humor and is weird in some way.

The world needs Mutants.

the formality scale

All communication is somewhere on **The Formality Scale**.

These are examples of...

Registers

"Register" is a linguistics term. It's the voice you use to talk, depending on who you're talking to.

Picture this: You're teaching a small group of people to play guitar. Which register should you use?

Slang/Jive
Example: Yo, check it. Uh!

Common/Informal
Example: Here's something you guys can use.

Formal/Corporate
Example: The subsequent technique shall be utilized by the student.

Use the Register that is *easiest and makes the most sense.* The answer is almost always Common/Informal. Unless you want people to laugh (either *with* you or *at* you), don't use Slang/Jive or Formal/ Corporate.

forced formality

On my freelance adventures, I've produced around 500 online music instructional videos — which means I meet a lot of fun, energetic musicians in Los Angeles.

They have a sense of humor. They can schmooze. (Of course they can… their careers depend on it.)

But once I point a camera at them, they discover they can't talk. They stumble, stutter, and select clunky phrases that don't make any sense.

Why?

All "stage fright" aside, it's because they're trying to force themselves to speak in a Formal Register, instead of just talking like a regular person.

Don't ever try to sound more educated than you are. You'll come off like Ben Affleck's character in *Good Will Hunting*:

> *"Since this is obviously not my first time in such altercations, let me say this: At the current time I am looking at a number of different fields from which to disseminate which offer is most pursuant to my benefit. These circumstances are mitigated. Right now. They're mitigated.*

Allegedly, what I am saying is your situation will be concurrently improved if I had two hundred bucks in my pocket right now. Now the business we have... here to for... you can speak with my aforementioned attorney. Good day gentlemen and until that day comes, keep your ear to the grindstone."

And never wear white athletic socks with a business suit.

Why So Smarmy?

Amateur writers think everything has to be written in a Smarmy register.

They think, "this is what writers write like."

It's because they've read a lot of bad writing.

> You don't want to be rich. You want to be responsible for lots of money.

Writers tend to be intelligent, eloquent, and they know what a Harvard Comma is. In high school, they couldn't play sports with their bodies, so they played them with their minds. It's the only way they could compete.

So the intention of their bad writing is to communicate one thing: "I know more about the English Language than you do."

It's the equivalent of Math Rock, which is: "I know more about Music Theory than you do."

Of course, they disregard the purpose of writing: To share an idea with a reader.

If you think someone you know (not you, of course) might be Smarmy, look for these warning signs:

- *But I digress.*
- *Ergo.*
- *Amongst.*
- *Indeed.*
- *Whilst.* (if they're not from the UK)

With that in mind, this book is mostly written in Common/Informal. I'm more Phil Rudd than Marco Minnemann, for those of you who like hitting things with sticks.

candles vs. wildfires

Trying to spread a weak message is like lighting individual candles on fire, one by one, and trying to keep them lit — but they keep going out.

A powerful message is like a California wildfire. It spreads, and you can't stop it.

Does your fire go out if you stop frantically running around and lighting the candles? Then maybe you should just let it go out. Maybe important fires will keep burning, whether you want them to or not.

"Mary Had A Little Lamb" didn't need to hire a PR firm.

lumpkin's law

Lumpkin's Law, named after the great business philosopher, Lance Lumpkin, states the following:

> *"The less valuable something is, the more it requires advertising."*

People put themselves through the agonizing process of making their art as boring and normal as humanly possible, and then wonder why they have to beg people to pay attention to it.

They get this idea that people will only like their art if it is bland. The result? Their art is bland. Yawn.

The corollary to Lumpkin's Law says:

> *"Great art sells itself."*

Or, if translated into Spanish, then into Chinese, and back to English again:

> *"A superior message advertises itself."*

If what you do is truly worthy, other people will pay attention and promote you. If what you do is remarkable, people will remark about it, spreading the word, and you'll draw a crowd.

Every time you say "Come out to my show" or "Buy my new album," what is the subtext? That no one actually wants to.

Self-promotion is the delicate art of subtext. If you talk the plot, it's over. It's tacky. Amateur.

Lance Lumpkin also said:

> *"If people aren't talking about what you've done, what you've done isn't worth talking about."*

Lumpkin was a womanizer and an alcoholic, but he was right most of the time.

the clown car of fame

These days, too many people want to be stars.

In previous generations, kids wanted to grow up and be a doctor or a plumber or a fireman. It's a shame, because only a certain percentage of the population can be famous.

Only so much room in this here clown car. Should I call for a clown limo?

how to be interviewed

When doing an interview, one bad instinct people have is to censor themselves.

So often I will find a person who is totally fascinating — a paradox, a brilliant mind. Turn on the camera, and suddenly they just want to be normal and hide the interesting parts of themselves.

To be an interesting person, you need depth. You need flaws, vulnerability. You need to surprise people. It's the unexpected that people are interested in.

The world is full of amateur artists who want so badly to make something important, to feel unique. And what do they do? They intentionally make boring art, and talk about it in a boring way.

"Goin' into the studio, you know? It's gonna rock. Big time. Totally psyched about it. Gonna record some new songs, it'll be killer, man. Check it out."

As soon as the camera is turned on, once they are having to commit to who they are, they lose that depth. They think it will make people like them.

No dark side = No interest.

What would happen if you went to see a movie, and there was no struggle?

> *"Once upon a time, everything was nice. There was a horse and it ran through the flowers and fields and everyone was happy. The end."*

They stand up a 2-D version of themselves and present that to the world.

> *"Here's my life-size cardboard cutout. See? I'm smiling. I'm doing great. Everything is great. You should like me now. Buy my stuff. It's great, too."*

It's the unusual cars with the dents in them that get names and personalities.

The same applies to people.

People don't form real connections based on all this two-dimensional, formal business babble. They finally become friends when they drop all the pretenses. When they're outside smoking a cigarette. Maybe they open up and complain about their problems. Aha! Now we see the real person!

Not everything should be measured numerically.

In Los Angeles, people are allergic to this. They keep up this stiff, formal, "everything is amazing" attitude. They like everyone, they like all music, everyone is a genius.

It's like we're all training to be talk show hosts, pretending to be fascinated by everything that everyone says. *"Wow!"*

Last I checked, it's illegal to say you don't like something, or that you're depressed, or struggling in any way. It's got to be the most emotionally repressed city in the free world.

Stub your toe, and you're exiled. *"You're never gonna make it here with that attitude!"*

break it

For something to be interesting, it has to be broken in some way. People are drawn to dissonance.

Like snakes, audiences can't see much detail, but they can track movement. To detect predators and prey, they're wired to pay attention to things that stand out from the background noise and break patterns.

Things that are normal are invisible. You don't want to be invisible, do you?

be specific

When someone (in an interview or in real life) asks you what you do, be specific.

Don't just give them a lot of vague meta-data, like dates and times and track lengths. *Everyone* is recording a new album. *Everyone* has a gig coming up. *Everyone* has a website.

This is your opportunity to tell your story — why what you do is different and special (even if only to you).

If it's not, why are you doing it?

points of interest

When you're trying to promote a product, such as a record, come up with your Points Of Interest.

Pretend it's going in *The Guinness Book of World Records*. Hit the high points. What is DIFFERENT about it?

As an example, here are the Points Of Interest from my Dr. Zoltan Øbelisk album, *"Why I Am So Wise, Why I Am So Clever, and Why I Write Such Good Songs."*

- A five-minute Drum Battle against virtuoso Marco Minnemann. Half of the drums were played by Marco on a real kit. Half were programmed one-note-at-a-time by Dr. Zoltan Øbelisk with *Cubase* and *Drumkit From Hell*. Can you tell which is which?
- This is the first time a record has featured pointillistic odd-tuplet drum programming with Drumkit From Hell as the lead solo instrument.
- Covers of Prokofiev, Bartok and Stravinsky, heavy rock style.
- Lalle Larsson contributed three polyrhythmic improv solo acoustic piano pieces.
- A five-minute violin solo by Paul Cartwright of *Battlestar Galactica*.

Granted, it was a bizarre, highly specialized album.

My point is, people don't talk about things that have stayed the same from day to day. It has to be the newest, the biggest, or the first of its kind.

going viral... and other clichés

Ah, the "Going Viral" cliché.

In order to "Go Viral" a video has to be something so outrageous and absurd that you can't help but spread it. It has to be something rare. Like an accident, someone getting hurt. Something that isn't usually captured on video. Something that no one has ever seen. Something strange and unfamiliar.

Everything that is successful is viral. "Viral" is just another word for the same old thing that has been happening for zillions of years. An idea that catches on and spreads throughout society.

Van Halen doesn't have to ask its fans to "please sign up for our mailing list and buy a T-shirt." If you have something unquestionably good, you will never have to do that. There needs to be a subtext — an unspoken, automatic gravity. You have to make something truly remarkable.

For something to "Go Viral," it has to be some combination of:

1. Easy to share/spread.

2. Easy to understand from beginning to end.

3. Surprising, unexpected.

4. Dangerous.

5. Never seen before, ever.

6. Taboo: "I really shouldn't be watching/listening to this."

That accounts for pretty much every media phenomenon ever.

What creates more interest, a celebrity singing a song, or a celebrity sex tape? The song is nothing but the context, the backstory. The sex tape is the story. You don't have a story until you add a twist or conflict.

Non-Celebrity Sex Tape — No one will watch it. No story. No conflict. Who? Why should we watch this?

Celebrity Song — Eh, OK. A bunch of people will listen to it.

Celebrity Sex Tape — EVERYONE will watch it. Now we have a story with context and conflict.

Here's a theory: Every time a celebrity goofs up (Ashlee Simpson's vocal track malfunction on live TV), it's staged.

Every "normal" career thing a celebrity does is nothing but a pretense, a backdrop, a setup for conflict.

Does anyone really want to watch a George W. Bush speech without mistakes in it? (OK, poor question.)

why do we care?

No one cares if a homeless person overdoses on drugs. But it becomes an earth-shaking headline when it's a celebrity. Why? Because it's surprising. It's dirty. Intriguing. Unsettling. "Why would he throw it all away?" Makes people think.

To concoct a pseudo-phenomenon, you can't be too edgy out of the gate. First you need your setup... to establish Point A. Then you can shock everyone and move to Point B. Otherwise no one cares about Point B. There has to be a story of change. Changing sides. Changing from good to evil. Changing from light to dark.

Live in the future.

An innocent child TV star isn't interesting. An innocent child TV star who grows up to lose all his teeth and sell his mom for crack is a story. There's irony. Drama. Do it right, and people will tell your story FOR YOU. It's free.

Point A: A beautiful picnic in the sun.
Point B: Ants. Giant ants. They burst out of the ground and kidnap your children.

Now people are paying attention. No one cares about a nice picnic going as planned.

People don't want to talk about the handsome actor. They want to talk about the bizarre space cult he joined. Is he out of his mind? Whoa! Hey, wait! It's not just him — lots of other famous people are into it. What the heck?! Now we have something to talk about.

How do you get in the news? Make a mistake in public. Make sure it's caught on video. The vice-presidential candidate with the most flaws and most conflict gets the most eyeballs. It's the "Can you BELIEVE this woman?" factor.

To be extremely famous, you have to create something that half the people in the world will hate, and half the people in the world will love. People love fighting, so they can't wait to fight over you.

Why does a Girl Who Can Play Guitar get a record deal? Because EVERYONE will want to talk about her, debate her talent, discuss the issue of sexual equality. How many times do you hear, "She's good... for a girl"? It creates conversation. It even got printed in a book.

Sales is not a bad word.

Here's another trick: Gossip is an incredible tool for promotion. How do you spread something all over town? Say it's a secret.

social media destroys hollywood

The Internet has taken First Place as The World's Biggest Delusion, a mighty honor once held by Hollywood.

Modern civilization has taken all of its finest narcissism and technology and handed it to amateurs. The problem is this: Few are doing anything important with it. The average Twitter user can potentially reach a quarter of this planet's population with a single Tweet. And what do they have to say?

"Didn't get enough sleep."

Maybe we should just get rid of the Internet and give everyone a 50-watt megaphone with a half-mile range for announcing their mundane status updates.

Before adding data to The Internet, you should define which form of online communication you intend to employ...

forms of online communication

Announcements: These are statements such as "Selling Lakers tickets, anyone interested?" or "Hosting a filmmaker panel tonight at 8." They communicate who/what/where/when data for those who are interested.

Open Queries: These are public questions, such as "Moving to Seattle next month. Can anyone recommend a physical therapist?" or "Seeking advice on buying my first guitar." These are intended to generate open commentary, discussion, or even debate. Very useful when you want to get feedback from multiple readers.

Your brain is a limousine.

Private Messages/Email: These are sent from one person to another. "Bill, are you available in June for collaborating on a blues album? I can pay your travel expenses" or "Sorry I couldn't make it last night. My uncle kept me on the phone for two hours, he is having a crisis."

Instant Messages: These are for immediate, active discussion, in real-time. These are convenient when you are at work and you want short bursts of conversation that do not involve talking on the phone.

Text Messages: These are most suited for instances when you want to locate someone in a loud concert, send a quiet reminder during a meeting, or to deliver a phone number or address to someone. For when simply using your voice is not an option.

Personal Journals: These are for keeping track of your own personal activities, thoughts and feelings, so that you can refer to them later for contemplation or analysis. "Went to store, started feeling better. Hoping I can go to Disney Hall tomorrow night," or "Thinking of eating some Pizza. Missing Kelly." No one needs to read these but you.

That means that Private Messages don't go on Walls. Personal Journals are not Announcements. Emails are not Instant Messages. Text Messaging is only a backup for when you can't or don't want to actually talk to a human.

Never post flirtatious or passive-aggressive little snipes or lobs that are intended to make people ask more questions. Streamline your messages and take into consideration who needs to read them and who does not. (This also goes for photos!)

Let's keep The Internet clean and organized, and save real, personal interaction for real people.

Thank you.

> The trick is to be a Cog in your own Creative Machine, instead of someone else's.

section 10:
will power, discipline and self-control

what is will power?

Will Power is all about that moment when you must be conscious, focus your intent, and do the right thing.

It's easy to let your consciousness drift off... to become a slave of habit, whim, or inertia. We all know what that's like.

It takes effort to pay attention. It's why it's easier to just watch TV.

Some extremists attempt to exist in a constant state of Mental Laser Beam. They make it a moral issue or lifestyle choice.

> *"Psychologically, the choice 'to think or not' is the choice 'to focus or not.' Existentially, the choice 'to focus or not' is the choice 'to be conscious or not.' Metaphysically, the choice 'to be conscious or not' is the choice of life or death."*
> — Ayn Rand, *The Virtue of Selfishness*

I find that exhausting, but the lesson here is: Wake up! The world would no doubt be better with fewer zombies.

the inconsistency of genius

1. Some days you'll be a genius.
2. Some days you'll suck.
3. (Actually, I lied. Most days you'll suck. Sorry.)
4. It's impossible to predict which kind of day it is.
5. Great art is the product of those few genius days.

This is why writers have the belief that you should write every day.

I agree. Show up every day and do the work, throw out the stuff that sucks, and you'll look like a genius.

get fired every day

You've been at it for years. No results.

How can you stay motivated? Learn from the daily reality of a telephone salesman.

Imagine calling 100 people a day and trying to sell yourself (or some product) to customers who don't want to hear from you. Out of those 100 phone calls, maybe one person will even talk to you.

The other 99 times you'll hear:

> *"No."*
> *"Let me think about it and get back to you."*
> *"Can you email me some information?"*
> *"Stop calling me."*
> *"Take me off of your list."*

And at the end of each day, even if you do a great job, you get fired. Because you're paid to wake up and look for work each and every day.

A salesman's entire career is spent unemployed, trying to find a job.

The flip side of this paradox is that a salesman is never unemployed, because he creates his own destiny. Think about that one.

Artists can learn a lot by hanging out with their shadow counterparts.

Everything is a haiku.

be aggressively responsible

Always look for new ways to be responsible.

When working for someone, always offer your input or new ideas. If they don't like your ideas, they won't use them. If they never use them, maybe you are working for the wrong person.

Take the initiative to solve problems for people without being asked. An intelligent and competent person will value this trait and want to work with you even more. A truly successful person will not blame their subordinates or partners when things go wrong — they see themselves as ultimately responsible for everything that happens.

Story trumps all.

Never work for someone who does not accept 100% responsibility for their own company. That is the risk a leader must take.

The danger in this? You don't want to step on toes. Mr. Incompetent doesn't want to lose his job.

section 11:
crash course in self-control

We don't have much time before the planet explodes, so here it is.

part 1: the body

"I can't stop myself from having another bucket of ice cream."

You mean you can't physically control your own limbs?

If I ask you to walk, can you walk? Can you stand up? Can you pick up a box?

Then why can't you NOT move your hand repeatedly in and out of that bucket of ice cream? What's stopping you? You can't control your own hands?

"I'm not an exercise person." Right. As if defining yourself as some alternate type of humanoid excuses you from motor control.

Stop pretending to be a helpless creature.

part 2: the mind

You say, *"I can't stop thinking about _____."*

Sure you can.

Here's a horrifying story:

I woke up one morning and felt something in my throat.

I tried to swallow it, thinking it was phlegm. I sat up in bed and gagged on it. An object was most definitely lodged at the back of my mouth. I panicked and ran to the kitchen.

I stood over the sink, trying to cough it up. Nothing.

I reached my fingers into my mouth and grabbed it — a slimy worm.

It wouldn't come out! Blood on my fingers. I gagged some more and pulled on it again. No luck. *Had a parasitical worm crawled into my mouth while I was sleeping?*

As I coughed and gagged, I ran to the bathroom, opened my mouth, and looked in the mirror.

It was my uvula, that hangy-thing at the back of my mouth. Swollen... and now torn from trying to yank it out.

> Amateurs worship technique above all else.

I went to the emergency room. It was a rare form of sore throat. It took about a week to heal. During that time, it would flap into my mouth if I talked.

Gross, huh?

There. I just controlled your mind. You were thinking about my story instead of thinking about ____.

My point is this: When you're busy, engaged in living life, and having real experiences (and real problems), you stop thinking about ____.

And no, it's not *Emotional Repression*. Focusing on bad things isn't more authentic and real than focusing on good things.

learn to say no

Let's get over this one right now.

Reasons you're scared of saying no:

1. Someone won't like you.

Maybe. Maybe not. The fact is, people often respect other people who say no. No is healthy. No is boundaries. No is strength.

2. You'll lose opportunities.

Eh. Saying no also creates opportunities. Why? Because you'll be free to focus your time and energy on what you really want, instead of what someone else wants.

Don't be a *doormat*.

Find a reason to say no today. Why? It's good practice. As you become more successful, people will want things from you. And you'll know just what to say.

lift weights with your mind

We like to believe that there is some magic trick or special secret to changing ourselves or achieving our dreams.

Often, there's not.

We spend money on therapy, we read Wikipedia, we play with Tarot cards. But sometimes we find there's no hidden answer to unlock. We like to think there's a shortcut, or that we're "getting ready" to change. These activities are mostly distractions.

Show me the panda.

We must do the mundane, obvious work that's in front of us.

It takes time and energy. Direct. Applied. Hands-on. Do it. Every day.

Like a muscle, your willpower will become stronger the more you use it. So go ahead and become a mental weightlifter. Weights will not lift themselves to achieve the results you want, and neither will your thoughts.

All of those years of slave labor will turn you into Conan The Barbarian.

the puritan work [my]thic

We are raised to believe that working hard for its own sake is a virtue.

I say it's not.

The purpose of work is to get results. Always ask yourself if you can get the same results without working hard.

Let go of the guilt. Achieve the results you want. Take the rest of the day off.

(Just kidding! You don't get a day off. Go solve the next problem!)

what is work?

You're not going to like this.

It's another one of my Helpful Delusions.

Here goes:

If you're doing something you enjoy, you're not working.

Sounds harmless, doesn't it?

You think it means, *"Do what you love, and you'll never work a day in your life."*

Nonsense. Every job, no matter what it is, involves some form of work. Whether it's working to staple booklets together in a factory, or working to suppress your boredom while stapling booklets together in a factory, something about it is going to suck.

Work is unpleasant. If you're not doing anything unpleasant, you're not making an effort. And if you're not making an effort, you're not changing. Without change, there is no life. Life necessitates change, effort, and unpleasantness.

Accept that life itself is a struggle.

Everyone, everywhere, is struggling against something. If you're an independent director-producer with a net worth of $3 billion, your struggle will be parenthood. You can't escape. Solve one problem and another will appear. It might be in another area, in another form, but it will always be there.

It's why storytelling is always the story of struggle.

Expect it. Welcome it in. Save it a seat.

Wherever you go, whatever you change into, you must always manage a healthy relationship with that polymorphous struggle.

make sacrifices

Sometimes it's possible to have two things at once, and sometimes it's not.

You've got to develop the wisdom to choose between conflicting options.

There's only so much time in the day, and you have a finite amount of energy. Maybe it's necessary to give up some "normal life" things that other people enjoy. Family, relationships, entertainment, possessions, nice car, etc. See if there is anything you can put aside and enjoy later.

Students do this all the time. They live like monks for many years so they can enjoy a better future. A sacrifice is not a failure.

A student asked drummer Simon Phillips: "What does it take, aside from talent and hard work?" His answer:

"Everything. You literally have to sacrifice everything to succeed on a global scale." (YouTube)

section 12:
mental health

maturity

What Is an Adult?

I spent the first 30 years of my life wondering what an adult is.

I think I've figured it out.

The core issue that kept me from becoming an adult was my refusal to accept the following concept:

No one else is responsible for me in any way.

That means physically, emotionally, financially. No one owes me anything. Ever.

Not parents, not friends, and certainly not the entertainment industry.

To be more specific:

If I die, and no one cares, that is perfectly fine.

It comes down to this: I can't expect anyone to care about me more than I do.

I have the ultimate responsibility to look after my machine. No one else is in my body or mind, so I am going to have to accept the job as Owner and Operator.

If you could climb inside a giant robot, where would you tell it to walk? What do you want to do with it? Would you tell it to work a boring job and come home and watch TV every night? Would you destroy its mechanisms by pouring sugar in its gas tank? Then why treat yourself like that?

And remember: Your friends and family have their own robots to take care of and drive around. That's their responsibility, so don't try to take over.

The Child Must Die

David D'Angelo has this catchphrase: "The Boy Must Die."

The same concept is talked about at length in a book called *King, Warrior, Magician, Lover: Rediscovering The Archetypes of the Mature Masculine* by Robert L. Moore and Douglas Gillette.

Adults are givers, creators of life. Children are needy takers. Parents are made for being eaten. Strange, but true.

Psychological Neoteny is what happens when the body grows into an adult but the mind remains a dependent child. One aspect of that is *caring what other people think.*

Adolescence is a time to rebel against your parents, teachers, and society. It's a time for forming your own identity apart from your original tribe. You must prove yourself worthy of survival, both physically and mentally.

If you don't do that, you will probably go through life seeing everyone external to you as an authority figure. You'll never trust yourself.

Being able to stand on your own and disagree with people is a sign of adulthood. Of course, learning to work with people despite your disagreements is another sign.

> **Professional does not mean formal and corporate.**

I Am Responsible

Instead of solving problems or answering questions for me, my old boss used to point at his head and say, *"Carl. I. Am. Responsible."*

Do not seek endless advice from others. No one else is the authority on your life path. Answering your own questions is the only way you will learn to trust your own mind.

The corollary is this: Don't blame your superiors.

It's easy to blame someone who has taken the responsibility of making decisions, but much harder to make decisions of your own. It is impossible to always make perfect choices, especially when you are in a position of having real power to affect a lot of people.

RTFM for your mind

So, you believe in Conspiracy Theories?

1. They found nano-thermite in the debris of the WTC.
2. The Unabomber was subjected to psychological brainwashing at Harvard.
3. Our world leaders are shapeshifting Lizardmen from another dimension.

Sure, it's all true.

But what's worse is that billions of people who have brains have never read The Owner's Manual.

Everyone should be required to study Logical Fallacies, Cognitive Biases, and Lateral Thinking. Let's talk about them.

Strong art affects people. If it doesn't, it's dead.

Logical Fallacies

Logical Fallacies are illogical arguments. They might seem logical on the surface, but they tend to involve mistakes through wordplay. Whenever you hear two people arguing, you'll hear a bunch of these.

Five examples:

Appeal To Law – Mistaking legal laws with morality. "If it's illegal, it must be wrong."

Begging The Question – This is an argument that is kind of circular. "Joe Satriani is an excellent guitarist, because his playing is superb."

Negative Proof Fallacy – When you're arguing with someone, and they ask you to prove that something is NOT true. "Can you prove that I am not an alien from outer space? I rest my case."

Package Deal Fallacy – Things that are often found together will always be found together. "People who live in Hawaii like to surf."

Reducto ad Hitlerum – "Hitler was a vegetarian, Hitler was evil, therefore being a vegetarian is evil."

There is also something called **Godwin's Law,** which states that *the first person to mention Hitler or Nazis automatically loses any argument.*

Did I just lose?

Cognitive Biases

Cognitive Biases are strange mental behaviors. Think of them as prejudices rather than simple logical errors. Check out these three:

Déformation Professionnelle – In 1966, Abraham Maslow said: "It is tempting, if the only tool you have is a hammer, to treat everything as if it were a nail." It's what happens, for example, when a guitarist only understands music through his experience with playing guitar — rather than understanding music from the perspective of another instrument, music in general, or the listener. *"Playing guitar on the guitar, instead of playing music on the guitar."* The term itself is a pun on the phrase "Professional Training." The remedy could be to study other instruments and art forms.

Money Illusion – This happens when the numerical value of money is mistaken for its purchasing power. In other words, wealth removed from meaning.

Semmelweis Reflex – Named after Ignaz Semmelweis, this is the tendency to reject new knowledge because it contradicts old knowledge. Mr. Semmelweis was the doctor who came up with the idea that hand washing prevented the spread of germs. Everyone thought he was nuts.

Lateral Thinking

Lateral Thinking is making leaps. It's solving a problem backwards or sideways. We ask questions we wouldn't normally ask. An answer occurs to us and we don't know why — but we follow it, and it works!

Because we've grown up with mathematics, logic, electronics, machines, we think our brain is completely sequential. We think everything has to be in order, and we have to walk through boring step-by-step rules to be able to get to the answer.

But we're complex machines that are built for taking shortcuts or leaps of insight. Call it Intuition, or whatever else is convenient.

The analytical method is often SLOWER than Lateral Thinking. We fear it because we consider it "illogical" and "irrational" and assume it's some sort of "cheating." Yet we were all born with it.

Some of the best Lateral Thinking takes place in dreams or while reading Tarot Cards. Comparing two seemingly unrelated concepts or symbols can lead to unexpected creative solutions.

People who consider themselves "technical" get trapped in a tiny, microscopic world with blinders on. They look through a tunnel of basic arithmetic.

When 2+2 doesn't solve the problem, they believe what they need is MORE Analysis, when in fact, they need to just stop stewing on everything and start taking wild guesses.

You'll be surprised how often the answer is right.

losing it

Creative people are prone to emotional problems. My theory is this: To have a breakdown, you need to have the machinery that can break down in the first place. *Congratulations, you are capable of Divergent Thought!*

I'm no doctor. I didn't go to medical school. But I've walked the earth in various stages of sanity and insanity for 35 years. If you believe you have a serious mental problem, please research and explore as many solutions as you can.

I'm only going to share my own perspective on Losing It.

Stage 1: Anxiety

For me, anxiety is the feeling that something is wrong, but I don't know what.

It's like my brain has to pee.

Maybe it's an urge to be creative, but not letting it out.

From experience, anxiety happens when I get bored and feel there's no meaning behind what I'm doing. I feel trapped, and that I'm working toward a dead end. It's really called "*Existential Anxiety.*"

Focus on the points of interest when promoting your art.

Just like our hands, I think our brains can get Repetitive Stress Injury. It's like Carpal Tunnel Syndrome of the Frontal Lobe.

In my own life, instead of treating anxiety with medication (I never have), it's worked to interpret it as a sign that *something needs to change.*

I imagine that inside me, I have a sort of Homunculus. He shares all of my body parts and senses. Yet he has no control. All he can do is nonsensically scream "ANXIETY!" at me, telepathically. Often, he knows something is wrong before I do!

It can get misinterpreted and misunderstood, it can seem wrong and overwhelming, but I think he is there to tell me: "WAKE UP!"

Unless anxiety manifests as debilitating physical symptoms (attacks), your dissatisfaction might be the best thing you have going for you. Use it.

Stage 2: Depression

If I don't listen to and act on my Anxiety, I end up Depressed.

This is my creative mind saying, *"I give up."*

Working from home, being alone all day, can drive some people crazy. I think it's the absence of pressure that gets to them.

Without coworkers and a boss to scrutinize you, it's too easy to not exercise, not take a shower, not take care of yourself.

I've considered that depression could be a part of Evolutionary Psychology. As far as we know, most of human history has been a miserable experience. We pooped all over ourselves. We had to actually hunt for food. We were miserable, smelly, filthy animals. When it rained, it rained on us and all our stuff got ruined.

It was a camping trip that lasted an entire lifetime.

Maybe we get depressed and anxious because for most of human history, that is how we have felt. Maybe it's hard to get over 250,000 years of bad living.

Depression Is Addictive

When I get Depressed, it's an Existential Crisis.

I deconstruct everything until it has no meaning. It engages my intellect. Makes me feel smarter than everyone. *"The humans are nothing but robots, and I'm the only one who realizes I don't exist!"*

Once I start expecting things to go wrong, I hope they *do* go wrong, so I can be right about it. It's like a drug. I get high off the Dark Side, like a Sith Lord.

Much of my creative output until I was 30 was fueled by depression, anxiety, and anger. It can really be inspiring.

Be careful with that stuff, because it can consume you.

A Vicious Web of Entropy

Depression is a mental state that reinforces itself. It's a Vicious Web of Entropy. Example:

When I'm depressed, I don't take a shower, and it makes me more depressed, which makes me less social, so I'm lonely, which makes me even more depressed, which keeps me from exercising, because I have no energy, which makes me even more depressed, which causes me to be irresponsible with my money, which makes me more depressed...

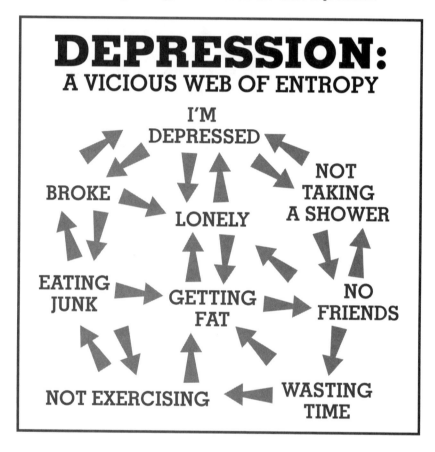

It will not stop until it has destroyed you.

Solution: Pretend You're Not Depressed!

One of my favorite tricks to beat depression is to pretend I'm not depressed.

It's simple and obvious — *but it works!*

It gets the ball rolling. Gets me out of the house and talking to people. It's the old Tony Robbins "Act As If" trick.

Take action:

1. Clean your apartment.
2. Take a shower.
3. Go for a jog.
4. Do some writing.
5. Listen to some Jim Rohn.

Sometimes depression was just passing through, like a really bad flu. Maybe you just needed a break from the routine. It's OK. As long as you beat it.

Get fired every day.

Control Freak

I meet a lot of paranoid and delusional people who struggle with their Creative Careers. They should all learn the essence of the Serenity Prayer.

Ever heard of it? Back in the early 1900s, there was a guy named Reinhold Niebuhr. In 1937, he wrote:

> *"Father, give us courage to change what must be altered, serenity to accept what cannot be helped, and the insight to know the one from the other."*

Alcoholics Anonymous adopted his quote and changed it to:

> *"God, grant me the serenity to accept the things I cannot change, the courage to change the things I can, and the wisdom to know the difference."*

My version goes like this:

> *"Some things you can control and some you can't. Figure it out, or you're one of THEM."*

A Creative Career is equal parts logic and illogic. Like a Flying Saucer, it's a machine with a lot of parts, and some of them will forever remain mysterious. Don't even try. The trick is to know when to expect it to make sense, and when you just have to trust it to get you into outer space without exploding.

Here's an example.

Right now, I have a comic book on my desk. I'm looking at the cover — and I think it sucks! If someone had asked me whether this art belongs on the cover of a comic book, I'd say NO. It's twenty superheroes standing together, expressionless. It's bland, there's no action, the characters have no personality. The colors are washed out. But the artist ended up with his work on the cover of *X-Men*, and I didn't!

In the end, the outcome is what matters. I can complain all I want about the bad acting on television, but they have a show and I don't. William Goldman said:

"In Hollywood, no one knows anything."

It's true. Everyone from your mom to Steven Spielberg has an opinion. They have different tastes, different aversions, different fears, different prejudices. Their minds can be calibrated differently in numerous areas. No one sees the same piece of art in the same way.

The scary news: The final judge (the general public) is not educated in the craft of entertainment. They haven't gone to school for music, film and art. They're essentially deaf, dumb and blind. Much of our work communicates to the unconscious.

If you take the robot apart and try to put it back together, it won't go.

An audience/reader/listener will get a vague sense of "that song was good" or "that movie sucked" but they cannot tell you why. Our meticulous craftsmanship makes little difference to them.

Example of things you can control*:
• Balancing your bank account.
• Cleaning your office.
• Washing your hair.
• Delivering a project on time.
• Buying the right gear.
• Paying your bills.
• How many MWP books you read.

Examples of things you can't control:
• If They like you.
• When They like you.
• What They will do to you.

Of course, even these things can go wrong. Accidents happen. As organized and efficient as we are, a giant asteroid could crash into our planet tomorrow, and we'd leave behind a bunch of unfinished errands.

There are some things you can safely bet on. If you hire Ben Burtt to create sound effects for your movie, he'll do a good job. You can control that. What you can't control is the movie's success. I don't care how many things you do right. If the audience doesn't love it, it's over.

Stop Watching the News

Out of all the human experiences throughout history, out of the hundreds of thousands of years we have been around on Earth, you think that something *that* important could have possibly happened in the past 24 hours?

The news is manufactured to scare you, upset you, keep you watching for longer so you'll have to watch commercials. Period. It's not worth subjecting your mind to all of that advertising, spin, and propaganda. If you really need to know if everything is OK, go outside and *look in the sky for mushroom clouds.*

Make a Physical Change

Here is a trick: Don't get caught up in your head.

If you want something to change, you must take a physical action in the real world.

Wash the dishes. Do some pushups. Move a pile of books. Go to a different place. Change your actual behavior.

Until then, nothing has actually changed.

There is a reason that we exist in a physical world... in a body, not just a brain.

Rearrange things.

Change your surroundings and you have taken action. Now things HAVE changed. Don't just say, "I want to change." That doesn't actually do anything. You must *take an action.*

Move your body.

If you're not moving your body, you're probably not changing anything.

Maybe this theory is not entirely true. You can probably find holes in it. But it's one way to change your life. It's one of my favorite Helpful Delusions.

Here's a short War Story:

When I moved to the West Coast in 2006, I just decided one day. I was no longer going to be where I was, in the same studio apartment, with the same desk. I saw that I was stuck.

My own brain had gotten me to where I was, and it was keeping me there.

I realized that if I kept on the same thinking pattern and kept doing the same things every day, I'd end up right where I was. More of the same. It's like a broken computer trying to repair itself.

Be aggressively responsible.

But I had this urge, just on the edge of my consciousness. It scared me. It was like a subconscious calling, telling me I needed to get out right away. And I did.

I left that day, and I stayed with my friend, on his couch. I left everything behind, right where it was. The next day I quit my job, and within ten days I was in a car headed toward the West Coast.

It's been almost four years now, and my life has definitely changed.

I am physically in a different place. In a different small apartment. In a different city. I have different friends. My diet is different. I have a new body. It's a new life. All because I made a PHYSICAL change.

I didn't just try to change my mind, or the way I thought.

So don't just sit there and focus on changing. *You probably won't.*

Integrate Your Identity

Be one person. Stop trying to present yourself in multiple ways.

> *"This is my professional Web page. This is my fun Web page. This is my random Web page."*

You'll probably just confuse yourself and think there is a major difference between elements that no one else perceives. It's hard enough to become successful once.

Integrating is all about integrity.

Be okay with who you are (and with people knowing who you are) all the time. The people (in business or in personal life) you really want to impress are smarter and more genuine than you think they are, and they understand that no one is a cardboard cutout.

Social Metaphysics: Games vs. Reality

Be able to differentiate between Games and Reality.

An example of a Game that has no direct relation to Reality is a College Class. Follow the rules, play the game, get the grade. You don't necessarily learn anything, but you get a credit. If you don't follow the rules, it's possible to learn everything but fail the class.

Social Metaphysics is the act of replacing our direct connection to the physical world with accepted social conventions. We have to be on the lookout for these types of substitutions.

Medicine isn't necessarily Healthy.
The News isn't necessarily Important.
Marriage isn't necessarily a Relationship.

Question popular definitions.

Some of us know there is something bigger than the fish tank we're born into. While most are content with this little world — swimming in circles, looking at the other fish, eating the food that is sprinkled on the surface — we're looking for a way to climb out and explore.

Take a Day Off

Take one full day off per week.

You will be more effective if you rest. It's true for bodybuilders and it's true for you.

Trust me.

Learn the difference between Talent and Skill.

section 13:
people

what the heck are friends?

■ 'm not sure anymore.
With some people, I do notice a few things:

1. They call me without "wanting something."
2. We have inside jokes.
3. They'll help me when I'm at my worst.

I believe the definition of a friend is always changing. Be ready for that.

Not everyone in the world is going to like you. *So what?* It is not your job to manage or control anyone else's likes and dislikes. Let them make their own decisions and dislike you if they want to. There are too many people out there to waste that much time on.

Try to read that sign on your back.

Just remember to be yourself. It is the only way to attract people who will appreciate you for who you are. You'll be a beacon, signaling for like-minded allies and warding off potential enemies.

friends are containers

I think it's possible that friends are pre-wired containers in our own minds that we fill with special energy.

In other words, maybe we already have a best friend, a mate, parents, siblings, teachers, heroes (and yes, enemies) in our minds.

126

It's just a matter of finding correlations to those things in "the real world."

There's an article in *The Onion*: "18-Year-Old Miraculously Finds Soulmate In Hometown."

You typically end up being friends with the people who happen to be around you. It's kind of **Phase 1**.

During my Phase 1, I grew up with a lot of people who didn't believe in me, didn't believe in themselves, didn't believe in the future.

That got old, so I moved on to **Phase 2:** I kicked 'em out and went looking for new ones. I created new friendships with wise and good intentions. Mutual benefit, good decisions, investing and receiving energy, seeing that energy that you invest turn into something bigger.

Take a day off.

Don't ever feel bad for growing beyond your old friends.

we are relationships

Here's one way to think about it: We are nothing other than relationships. In fact, we *are* relationships. You are what you are because of what you are relative to someone else.

If you hang around with people who make you feel smart, you'll experience *smartness*. Be sure to relate to the right people.

alienation is good

The more highly-specialized your interests, the fewer people will share those interests. The more you learn about a topic, the fewer people will know that information. That's all OK. That's the price you pay for being an expert.

Creative people are a minority. For the sake of following our passions, we might do things that others don't consider normal. We seem to know way too much about things that aren't joked about on sitcoms.

It's OK to spend a lot of time alone. Most creative people do.

the illusion of status

Do not place yourself below anyone.

No matter how much fame, money, freedom and material resources someone else may have acquired, accept that you deserve to have the same, and take your own path as seriously as they do. What you do is just as valid and real. Which means that what everyone else does is also valid and real.

Calm down.

Status is only determined by the ruler you're using to measure.

Those television actresses in Beverly Hills aren't rich compared to the King of Saudi Arabia, Abdullah Bin Abdulaziz Bin Abdulrahman Bin Faisal Bin Turki Bin Abdullah Bin Mohammed Bin Saud.

Remember, a person of authentic value does not need to display status, fame or wealth.

personas

When you meet someone for the first time, you're only seeing what they want you to see. You're only interacting with a mask, not a person.

Your health is your time is your energy is your life.

You need to get past that baloney.

Break through it. *Somehow*. Get them to relax.

Businessmen act stiff.

Writers act intelligent.

Artists act dreamy.

Musicians act stupid.

Actors act... like you.

It's a lot of role-playing.

Mostly because they're afraid. They're trying to impress you.

If someone you know is perfect all the time, you don't really know them. Real people are flawed and vulnerable. Cardboard cutouts are not.

It is very difficult to work with someone who is a two-dimensional cartoon superhero 24/7.

Getting to know someone is a process of unmasking — for both of you.

Maybe you need to be the first one to drop your guard. (At your own risk, of course.)

acting in real life

All of that being said, you can learn a lot by role-playing.

I used to enjoy public pranks. Pretending to be someone I'm not. Seeing how much I could fool people.

In 2000, my friends and I dressed up in business suits, flew to New York City, rented a space at a technology convention, and marketed a new invention that didn't exist. We called the device (and our company) D.E.M.I. — Digital Electronic Media Incorporated. We had a fake story about how we discovered a strange contraption in a mad scientist's garage. We printed up blueprints and brochures detailing it, and we claimed it was simultaneously a File Compression Format and Stand-Alone Peripheral Device. It would revolutionize the music industry if we could just get the funding together.

Over the course of the weekend we practiced our pitch, and the mythology grew. We claimed we didn't have the device with us, because it had to be tested on the Salt Flats of Utah.

The people at the expo couldn't distinguish us from the rest of the pretentious "music Internet" companies, who were actually serious. Investors wanted in. A reporter from *The New York Times* wanted to set up an interview with us. As soon as people would turn their backs, we'd toss their business cards over our shoulder and go to work on the next sucker.

Sure, it's lying. But it was for a good creative cause, and *no one got hurt*.

You can also get away with a lot on the Internet. You can really be anyone you want. It's liberating. Just "don't believe your own press," as they say.

mind your own business

People are not as concerned with what you are doing as you think they are. If they are, it just means their own lives are boring and they are wasting energy.

To make it even more complex and postmodern: *Don't waste your energy paying attention to people wasting their energy.*

The point is, you don't need to care what other people are doing. You're a unique person with a perspective. The more you can write from that perspective, the more powerful a statement you'll make.

Every person is a different camera pointed at the world. If your camera is just like everyone else's, that's boring.

Use your weird camera. It's what makes you unique.

the pretense of fame & popularity

There is a large degree of mutual pretense between star and fan.

Ask yourself if you need to "pretend" to be what you are, or if you simply are.

Are there many behaviors that you take on simply because you want to project your pretend identity?

Many celebrities are overcompensating. They've left their dark or mundane past behind and are inventing their future out of thin air. You can move to Los Angeles and pretend to be anything you want. But there is a dark side to that.

I quit music because I couldn't handle all of the pretense I had to keep up. There's too much social nonsense associated with the act of making music.

In 2006, a subculture of strange music fans cared who I was. I made an album with some reputable musicians on it, and it got some good press.

On one occasion, I was recognized by a young girl in a hotel in the middle of nowhere, Pennsylvania. Her dad asked if I could pose for some pictures with her.

I didn't even have enough money to get a hotel room that night, and almost had to sleep in my rental car. I had to call my mom back in Florida and ask her to transfer money into my bank account. How embarrassing is that?

I was answering daily fan mail from kids asking for advice. I didn't have any advice to give them. I didn't know what I was doing. I felt like such a phony.

Beware of people with bad ideas and money.

I couldn't handle the pressure of the pretense that not only I invented, but which everyone mutually assumed. There is an inferred lifestyle and level of power or success that goes along with it all, even on such a small scale. It was exhausting to maintain the illusion.

the delusion of infinite scale

Don't build a bloated, impersonal machine. Keep it small (or a proper size). Serve the outcome.

Too many people have this infinitely scalable hope that they'll just keep getting bigger and bigger. And that there's something wrong if you don't want to.

You should want to monetize everything, right? The bigger the better? Phh.

How big of an audience do you actually NEED? Do you NEED to sell 500,000 copies of something when there are only about 1,000 people on the entire planet actually interested in it?

Stop watching the news.

Why try to force it?

Too many people start with fame and fortune and work backward. It's as if everything is created these days with the intention of being a mainstream blockbuster. It's absurd.

Don't try to over-scale your audience. Don't overestimate the importance of everything you do. You'll just look silly and annoy everyone.

A schoolteacher might only have a class of 30 students. Maybe less, depending on the type of class. What's wrong with that?

Figure out how many people are going to be interested, and focus on reaching those people.

Congratulations, you've made it.

Google the theory of *1,000 True Fans* by Kevin Kelly.

people are broken machines

Working with machines is easy. At the end of the day, they DO follow logic.

People don't.

The job of a technician or programmer is to think as clearly and logically as possible all day long in order to solve problems. They know that their machines run on logic.

This doesn't work with people. Half of the work their brains do is irrational.

If there are people involved with your work, most of your time will be spent on their mental problems, hacking their consciousness to get them to sort of do what you want.

You press a key and the human says, *"I don't want to. I'm upset today."*

Despite what you have experienced, if you buy a good computer with a stable OS and good software, it will work most of the time. If it doesn't, you can often fix it by rebooting or reinstalling or simply buying another one. In that case, the answer is simple and logical. You can usually troubleshoot and solve it.

> **People who talk the most have the least going on.**

But people problems don't always have a logical solution. Solving their errors might have something to do with what kind of chair they are sitting in because it's not as nice as someone else's chair that they saw in a movie, what their boyfriend said to them about their feet last week, or if they just don't trust people named Bob.

How are you supposed to know what is going on in their chaotic minds?

I don't know. No one does. As Dr. Lacking says, "It's almost as if they're *individuals*."

management/leadership

If the universe decides you need to be punished for your crimes in a previous life, you might find yourself as the leader of a creative team. Maybe it's a band, or a group of writers, or an improv group.

The leader of a creative team must:

- Be in the trenches.
- Take all ideas and suggestions seriously.
- Be patient.
- Never tolerate trolls.
- Value the success of the project above his own power.
- Propose the best course of action, not dictate it.
- Wrangle creative people and keep them on schedule.
- Do the random work that's left over.
- Recognize the contributions of his team.
- Get results.

We've all worked day jobs and had awful bosses. Remember how they made you feel? Inferior. Worthless. Helpless. Mechanical. Empty.

Do the opposite. Empower everyone.

A creative team is no place for Tools and Cogs. You're thinking of a fast-food restaurant. And this isn't one of those. Right?

how to hire famous people

In 2005 I got a bunch of (kinda) famous people to be on my musical album. Musician kids ask me how I did it.

Easy. Remember the following:

1. Most pro musicians, as long as they're not superstar artists, are working session players. As long as you can pay them *something* and what you're hiring them to do won't be *embarrassing*, they'll probably agree. Email them... and try at least *three times* before you give up. It took me three times to get a reply from Virgil Donati.

2. Once you get one involved, you can get as many as you want. It's like a secret handshake. Suddenly you're *in*.

3. Give them an opportunity to do something they don't usually do. Let them "have fun with it," as Anders Mouridsen says.

4. It helps if your project is really strange. I got a lot of great performances on my album for free because other artists respected my oddball vision and just wanted to be a part of it. Never underestimate the power of doing something different!

5. As with anything else, you'll hear "no" (or get no reply) more often than you'll get a "yes." Keep knocking.

communication

We'll keep this simple, just like all communication should be.

Fundamentals:

1. Always communicate on an intellectual AND AN EMOTIONAL level.

2. Don't try to sound smarter than you are. You'll get busted.

3. If the reader (or listener) doesn't understand, you have failed.

4. A conversation is two people talking and listening to each other.

5. Talking to dogs is fun, especially when they cock their heads.

Don't live the life of a handicapped person. You have a body that works. Use it.

how to live in the imaginary city

the 13 commandments

'**ve collected a few bits of counter-intuitive wisdom, which will be useful if you ever find yourself in Los Angeles.

1. **It doesn't actually exist.** It's a sprawling collection of little towns, with an imaginary city projected on top of it by its delusional residents. Those who "live in Los Angeles" will compete and argue about its physical boundaries, when it actually has none.

2. **There are many diet fads to choose from.** The most popular is Cannibalism.

3. **The people who talk the most have the least going on.** If someone is talking to you, they either want money, or they want you to introduce them to someone with money.

4. **Speaking of money, lending it out is a fantastic idea, especially if you never want it paid back.** Everyone here happens to be on the verge of something really incredible and

life-changing. Think of Los Angeles as a Gamblers Anonymous convention.

5. **Crime is imaginary.** I've lived here four years and have never seen a shootout with machine guns, a helicopter exploding, or Sandra Bullock and Keanu Reeves launching a city bus across a gap in a highway. I heard a theory that all the murders and gangs and drugs they portray in movies about L.A. are just scarecrows to keep more people from moving here.

6. **It's impossible to make friends.** This is mainly because Los Angeles has no people, only IMDb profiles.

7. **We all know or are related to someone in a band, on TV, or in magazines.** More likely than not, if you move here, you will work in or on the periphery of the entertainment business.

8. **Los Angeles is an infinite hallway with doors on each side.** The only ones that will ever open for you are the ones that are mislabeled.

9. **It's a capital crime to have a negative thought.** If you stub your toe and curse, you'll be blacklisted by every commercial agent and producer in town.

10. **Don't believe anything until it's already happened.**

11. **Beware of The Surrogate Industry.** These are small businesses set up to capitalize on people trying to "make it." Consultants, producers, promoters, managers, gurus, mentors, coaches. They're mostly people who couldn't make it themselves, so what do they know? You're better off buying your own deck of Tarot Cards. If you're cheap, *www.llewellyn.com* has a free online spread.

> Integrate your identity — it's hard enough to succeed as one person.

12. **It is entirely impossible to predict who or what will be successful (or for how long).** Since there are no rules, it's actually impossible to make a mistake. The odds are in your favor that, if you stick with it, you will achieve some, if not all, of your dreams.

13. **Never take Los Angeles seriously.** The people who "get it" are the ones who come here to gamble, not to live. If you can someday leave Los Angeles having achieved *anything positive*, you've won.

If you can accept the ironic fun in these "commandments" then you are ready to visit Los Angeles for the weekend. Bring a sense of humor, your best handshake, and plenty of antiemetic… and you'll be great!

three types of people in los angeles

I'll keep this brief.

There are three types of people in Los Angeles, and they happen to rhyme.

Makers.

Fakers.

Takers.

Makers create authentic value with their talent and skill.

Fakers pretend to be Makers, and often succeed.

Takers get rich off the other two.

Decide which of these you are. There's room for everyone. Just so you know, the Fakers and Takers far outnumber the Makers.

Get the website out of the way.

Makers sometimes end up as Fakers, which is silly.

I really believe that everything happens because of Makers. We should all strive to be one for as many hours a day as possible.

building a time machine so i can kick my own ass

I can tell you this with 100% sincerity:

Moving to Los Angeles is the best decision I have ever made.

For the first 30 years of my life, I knew I was in the wrong place. Every bone in my body was screaming it. In fact, I am convinced that most of the unhappiness I experienced while living in Florida was due to Suppressed Ambition.

With the money I make from book sales, I hope to build a time machine, so I can go back in time and kick my own ass. Thank you.

part 2:
them

section 1:
why freelance?

I t's time to get practical.

Besides, we're running out of pages.

Why Freelance?

1. No commute, no uncomfortable shoes.

2. Keeps your technical skills sharp.

3. You can fire your boss at any time.

Before I went freelance, my Monday–Friday day looked like this:

6:15 – 7:00 wake up

7:00 – 7:30 shower and put on tie, uncomfortable shoes

7:30 – 7:45 curse, stomp around

7:45 – 9:00 ride bus or train

9:00 – 6:00 sit at a desk

6:00 – 7:15 ride bus or train

7:15 – 8:00 eat, take care of things that weren't taken care of during the day

Fourteen hours — *fourteen fraking hours!* — of my awake time were spent either at work for someone else, preparing to work for someone else, or traveling to and from work for someone else. The worst part is that my existence was consumed by following orders and suppressing my mental facilities, making someone else rich. That's insane!

It's considered normal to live that life, but it was never for me.

The music is not in the notes.

As much as everyone around me thought I was out of my mind, *quitting my day job during a recession was a GREAT idea.*

Employee Mindset: I have a life, but I don't know what to do with it, so I rent it out to someone else. Bring it back when you're done with it.

Now I'm self-employed. Every morning I interview myself. I promise I'll pay me at the end of the month if I prove I can do a good job. Then I buy the company, work all day, and fire myself before going to bed. After 30 days of that, I send myself a bill.

my results

In 2010, one of the worst economic years in U.S. history, **I made $70,000 working part-time from home.** (It sounds like a cheap spam email, but it's true.)

No, it's not a ton of money per year. But it translates to about **$70 an hour** for my time. It's more than I made at any full-time day job that consumed my life. And I did it without wearing those uncomfortable shoes. In fact, I did it wearing *no shoes.*

Could I have made more money? Yes. In fact, I turned away a lot of work.

Why?

Because I value my free time, and the time it takes to develop my own creative projects. I like to spend my time daydreaming, going for long bicycle rides, and studying.

I don't want to work full-time for other people. That would make me an employee, wouldn't it?

excuses: but the economy sucks!

Let's all agree on one thing: The News (television, paper, online) doesn't exist to deliver relevant information on current events. It exists to sell advertising. Its job is to control your eyeballs. Period.

They will publish anything that:

1. will keep you reading/watching/listening, and
2. won't result in a lawsuit.

Like all video games (laboratories), the points (dollars) add up when the players (rats) click the correct combination of buttons. In this case, those buttons are:

1. Contagious diseases.
2. Wars.
3. Celebrity deaths.
4. Natural disasters.
5. Sex scandals.

Shuffle them up, and you've got The Formula. Ka-ching! Anything else is either:

1. Advertising, or
2. Utilitarian filler, to give the impression of substance.

But that's not what keeps The News in business.

If it's flashed in front of them, most people will pay attention to sex, drugs, violence and money. (You know, a typical Tarantino movie.) It's a perfectly natural reaction. We're wired for it.

So, when all four of the above topics run dry, The News announces that The Economy Sucks.

Ouch, my wallet! My 401(k)! The sky is falling!

Humans have lived on this planet for 250,000 years, most of those without any of these modern contraptions. Go complain to a caveman. See if he cares.

Until the planet is destroyed, be a good cockroach and get back to work. Someone, somewhere, has your dream job. Don't let The News tell you what's impossible.

Lose everything, many times.

who to work with

I like to work for... ahem... WITH artists and small businesses.

1. They're excited about their projects.

2. Usually only one decision-maker.

3. More creative than working with a corporation.

Working for cool people is probably more important than the actual work I do.

There, I said it.

I don't do work. I help cool people achieve their dreams.

They don't dream of paying someone to program standards-compliant HTML/CSS code. They dream of having their own place on the Internet, having a .com after their name, and expressing their ideas. Always work for cool people who have dreams.

There is only one reason to talk on the phone: When the Internet is broken.

section 2:
workflow/
organization

organizing your space

a rule of thumb: If you don't use it, you can't see it. Put everything that serves no function in the closet. Better yet, sell it.

There's nothing wrong with a few decorations. A plant. A painting. A statue.

Random cable adapters, stacks of junk mail, dirty clothes and pretzel crumbs don't count.

You won't use it later. I promise.

gmail as to-do list

Gmail is incredible. Here is how I use it:

- Gmail is my To-Do List.
- If something is in my Inbox, that means it requires Action.
- Any email that doesn't require Action goes away: it gets Archived.

Simple. I don't want to flip through pages and pages of things I've already read, things that serve no purpose, things that don't deserve my attention.

As I write this, it's a Thursday morning. I have four emails in my Inbox.

One is a strange email from a fan. I plan to read more of it before archiving it.

One is a response from a voice actor. I keep it there to remind me that I need to take action. I want to schedule a recording session with him, but I need to look through my scripts first.

One is a newsletter from *Creative Screenwriting* magazine that I intend to read in detail.

One is from a Web design client. He sent me some updates.

don't call me

In my world, there is only one reason to talk on the phone: When the Internet is broken.

If there's business to be discussed, or technical details, I want it in email. Why?

1. There's a searchable info trail. There can be no debate later about who said what. I don't want any confusion in my factory.
2. It requires us to articulate our thoughts and think things through before communicating. I like to think before I talk.
3. If I am discussing technical details with someone over the phone, I'm required to type notes, which is redundant work. If the info was sent to me in email, I already have notes.
4. It saves time. It's too easy to get caught up in gossip and social metaphysics.
5. The phone is an interruption. It's like a dog that sits in front of the TV and stares at you.

Unless you're a close personal friend, I won't answer.

When I'm working on a project, I'm all-in. It takes effort to build up momentum. I am less effective when I am scatterbrained and interrupted.

You are your most important client.

Throughout the day, I switch from screenwriting to video editing to Web programming to analyzing music.

For fast and high-quality work, I need to do one thing at a time.

Here is a real-life example. Which is better?

• 8 hours working while goofing around, or
• 2 hours working, then 6 hours to do whatever you want

I'm an introvert. For me, talking to humans requires a special type of patience and advanced weaponry. It's expensive to rent and dangerous to activate. Keep the humans out of the factory so the robots can work.

The only way phone is any better than email these days is if you want to size up a person or get a feel for their personality. Otherwise, just use email.

Calling someone these days is the equivalent of walking into their office and standing in front of their computer screen. "HI, I'M HERE." I get rid of people who call me, either by training them to email me, or just not answering.

email me

Rules:

1. Make your emails elegant, like Haiku poetry.
2. Don't repeat yourself. (Or rephrase a previous statement, like I am doing right now.)
3. Don't do too much glad-handing and back-slapping.
4. Don't send emails from your iPhone unless it's something that needs an immediate answer.
5. Dedicate 15 or 20 minutes each night to focus on writing emails. Capitalize your sentences.

giving instructions

- When you give instructions, send bullet points.
- Like this.
- Be specific and concrete.
- There are five items on this list.
- See how easy it is?

Do not do this:

I was looking at Element #1, and gee-willikers, it sure did seem like it was a little too dull. I was thinking, maybe if you have the time, could you try something more subtle and rich? It seems lifeless and cold. I want it to POP, so could you experiment with making it more prominent, but not intimidating, as this is the most important element on the page, that everyone is going to LOVE and CLICK ON. Also, do you have any ideas for putting it somewhere else on the page, somewhere less timid yet firm and unassuming, maybe re-writing all of the code and re-sizing all of The Other Elements, in case Element #1 might seem even more confident if we swapped the order... maybe try Element #3 in Color #5, something more active and inviting, and then Element #2 in the original color and see how that looks? I was also wondering about the business card. Element #4 should definitely go on top and be in Color #2, I think that would seem so much more curious. Have you made any progress on the other project? Also, on the other one, just keep it the same, but also try something in between the colors of Element #1 and Element #4, something more unique. Or else we can just skip that one and go back to the previous version before the last one, when it was better. By the way, on the other page, or for a second option for this one, can we try something more subdued, but keep the rest just like the previous email I sent you? Then make Element #2 less aggressive, then let's go ahead and add a second Element #1, but change the size of it, so it won't clash, and let's make everything Horizontal. What do you think? Heck. On second thought, forget about that. We don't need to do that. What was I thinking? I think it's all fine the way it is, but again, can we try to make the color of Element #1 more fresh and crisp but not so in-your-face? So just those 4 changes, on both of the ones that are like this, and we're done!

Do this:

Change color of Element #1 to Orange. Attaching a sample. I'm also mailing you a bonus check for $5,000 because you're awesome.

Done!

Too often, I have to wade through (not kidding) 500–1,000 words with the instructions vaguely hidden between chunks of personal rambling. As I've said before, people who type a lot don't know what they want.

When I am working, I don't have time for all that. The meter is running!

If you don't know what you want, then stop typing and start thinking. Or, shut up and let me do a great job for you.

how to name your files

If you're going to send a file to someone, DO NOT name it like this:

thing.zip

Or like this:

da filez 4 u ok thx.zip

Or like this:

yo fo'shizzle whatup bam.zip

Put yourself on the World Showcase.

This isn't a place to be funny or cute. Just do it like this:

CarlKingCreative_GuitarTracks_IbanezCommercial.zip

Always attach your name to your files! The longer and more descriptive the name, the better. I use underscores and title case to separate its parts. When the file is downloaded to a cluttered desktop, it will be easy to find. If you're submitting creative materials to someone that you don't know, this is particularly important. You want the person to mentally link the file to your name. You want them to be able to look you up.

Tip: In addition to putting your name in the file name, always TAG your MP3 files. I've had kids email me random MP3 files with no tags. They're still in my iTunes library, but heck if I know who made them. Remember that tags can get lost, so do everything you can to make sure your name is associated with what you do.

thrown fights

Freelancing for the wrong people can be like thrown fights in boxing. *You're paid to lose.*

When the client doesn't trust me, I feel like a boxer who is ready to get out there in the ring and kick my opponent's ass, but I have a simpleton coach who doesn't know the first thing about fighting.

The contradiction, of course, is that my coach is the one who pays me, so I have to do what he says and keep losing fights, getting my butt kicked. Because in this loony bin, winning or losing the fight isn't what's important, it's more about the coach and his preferences that matter in this equation.

That's how clients sometimes turn into nothing but "financial fertilizer." Some clients come to me, hire me, and I lose over and over again, seeing the bad ideas happen every step of the way. But they don't care. It makes them happy. Makes them feel good that we *suck*.

task inertia

Switching tasks wastes time and energy.

When I'm running my video editing factory and I have ten projects in the pipeline, I line them up like this and group all similar tasks:

- Audio cleanup.
- Multi-camera cuts.
- Titles.
- Exporting.
- Encoding to Flash.

Which means, I do the audio cleanup for ALL TEN before moving onto the next task.

Why? By the time I'm on the third batch of audio cleanups, I've increased my speed through repetition. It's why assembly lines are so efficient.

Try working "out of order." See how much time it can save you.

diminishing returns

In everything there comes a point where the amount of energy you invest stops yielding a substantial return. I remind clients of this. Some of them like to fidget and tweak the smallest details — stuff that no one will ever notice.

wabi-sabi

The Japanese have a concept called "Wabi-sabi," which refers to the transience and imperfection of all things. Everything is in motion, things are being made or destroyed, we're all in a constant state of change.

If you don't want to be upset for the rest of your life, you must remember that things are made to serve a purpose — not to be flawless. In a way, craftsmanship is kind of irrelevant. Make it across the finish line, get the trophy. Earn a living.

When you write a book, half the stuff people read in it isn't even what you actually wrote. Their imaginations are filling in all the conceptual gaps. It's all filtered through opinion and prejudices. You're not even really reading the words on this page right now. You're only seeing the concepts. You're not analyzing each and every letter, every curve on the typeface. Check out that nutcase named Plato if you don't believe me.

Life really is an imitation. I believe that.

Everything in this world is a knock-off of something that is perfect. At the same time, perfection is itself an illusion. (Boy, am I getting myself in trouble.)

Because of that paradox, don't try to get everything right. Everything is a rough run-through with the band, before the show. A dress rehearsal. You'll miss some of your cues, but just get out there and go.

We all have our own threshold of detail we can perceive through our senses. It might be fun to criticize those poor souls listening to Nickelback, but it's not necessarily a moral issue.

I can't tell $10 wine apart from $100 wine, and I don't care to… but if a musician's timing is anything short of metronomic, I plug my ears in disgust.

Writers like to argue about "toward" vs. "towards." Does it really matter? Really? (Sorry, Strunk and White.)

done is the engine of more

Bre Pettis and Kio Stark wrote *The Cult of Done Manifesto* in 20 minutes (because [they] only had 20 minutes to get it done).

It consists of 30 philosophical points on productivity that sound a whole lot like the ancient concept of Wabi-sabi. It's brilliant. Google it.

outrun the bear

Two campers are walking through the forest when they suddenly encounter a grizzly bear.

The bear rears up on his hind legs and lets out a terrifying roar.

Both campers are frozen in their tracks.

The first camper whispers, "I'm sure glad I wore my running shoes today."

"It doesn't matter what kind of shoes you're wearing, you're not gonna outrun that bear," replies the second.

"I don't have to outrun the bear, I just have to outrun YOU," he answers.

[Source: unknown.]

section 3:
business

keep the meter running

always run a time clock program and log your hours.
I use Harvest. (*getharvest.com*). It's $12 a month.

When you're working for someone, it doesn't matter if it only takes you a few minutes to fix something. Punch in and out.

For example, if you do websites, you might end up with a client who will nitpick a website to death. Every day they'll have a pesky task for you to do.

Add those up and at the end of the month you've got 150 minutes to bill them.

Remember that time is valuable. You might end up with people who are friends, asking you to do work for them. And that's fine. In return, ask them to come over and wash your car, clean your toilets, take your dog for a walk. Let them experience it. Because seriously, ten hours of work takes ten hours.

Sometimes free time is priceless.

People don't understand the value of time until they've volunteered it.

I always charge for what I call "Project Management."

When someone calls me, if I am reading someone's email, and if I am even thinking about their project, *I charge for it.*

I don't charge per Widget. I charge for my attention and focus.

150

If you want me, you've got me 100%. I don't answer the phone. I don't read other emails. I am sitting there and staring at your website design.

When that clock isn't running, my desk is clean and I'm at home, doing whatever I want. I don't care about your project when I am playing with my dog.

I ask myself what is worth it to me? I sell my time and attention. No, I don't rent it. Because if you're renting something out, you get it back at the end. Nope, it's used up. Gone. I don't get my time back.

The time I spent on your mockup is time that is gone forever. That hour I spent on fixing your code could have been spent *enjoying myself.*

For that hourly rate you get a creative mind that has been trained for decades. I've spent that time studying every aspect of the creative process. I've trained myself how to recognize patterns and assemble them into creative works. And now you will pay me to NOT work on my own projects, to NOT live my own life.

See through the cheese.

The reason you're paying me is because it's something you don't want to do, and it's obviously something I don't want to do, either, or I'd do it for free.

what should i charge?

I charge two separate rates. I recommend the following ranges (as of 2010), depending on who you work for:

Amateurs/Independent Artists: $20–$35/hr.
Professionals/Corporate: $50–$100/hr.

I charge the same hourly rate for updates, redesigns, maintenance, and whatever else they want.

But don't be too strict about it. Sometimes it's hard to figure out which rate a client deserves to pay.

Don't worry. *You'll know soon enough.*

should i ask for a deposit?

I don't ask for deposits or down payments. A few reasons for this:

1. I don't need it. I'm so busy with work that I can afford the disintegration of any project.

151

2. I like to get paid AFTER I've done the work. Otherwise, there's no financial payoff at the end of a project, and it feels like I'm working for free the whole time.

3. If my client would be happier going somewhere else part of the way through a project, I encourage it.

diversify your income

The great thing about working freelance is that you can diversify your income.

You can avoid putting yourself in a position where a single person has power over your livelihood.

The more diversified your income sources, the more freedom you will have to walk away from any situation, and toward the things you want to do.

what about *pro bono*?

Look at the big picture and realize what sorts of additional opportunities or benefits can come out of any situation. Work for cheap or free sometimes. Help other people out with their projects. Accept help, too.

Nothing wrong with that, if you want to.

referrals: the magic word

"Referrals" is the magic word. Really.

I have never, ever done any advertising for my freelance services. I have a website with samples of my work, but I have never looked for work.

It all started with **a single client.**

A good friend of mine, Zeke, wanted me to help him with a fun website. We designed it while sitting on his couch in Venice, California, in exchange for pizza. I didn't even really know what I was doing back then. But he was thrilled, and he referred me to his coworker, Tamar.

I made a website for her, and she became the biggest loudmouth promoter of my services that could ever exist. The best person to ever work for, period. Don't steal her from me.

For the past two years, I've suffered through endless business based only on word-of-mouth. I've picked up about 50 paying projects, just because I did a great job on that first free website.

getting started

The best advice I have for getting started and finding clients is this:

Intern for your own creative studio. Work for free. Build a kick-ass portfolio.

If you want to design websites, find five musician/filmmaker/actor friends who need a site. They're everywhere. The artist website market is endless, especially in Los Angeles. There's another band forming or student film being made every ten minutes.

You don't need to be an expert. Learn as you go. No one will complain, because it's free. Just make five simple artist sites. In the process, you will probably encounter just about every major problem imaginable. Most of the good Web design books will get you up to speed in no time.

Just get the factory running. Build a hurricane of busy-ness around yourself. People will get sucked into it and start paying you.

Once you're in, you're in.

getting paid

I never worry about it.

As of mid-2010, in the two solid years I've been free-lancing this time around, I've only had one client skip town.

Did I mind? No.

Focus the majority of your time and energy on activities that are consequential to your future.

I've had other clients overpay me, refer me to their friends, and help me with my own projects. I don't focus on the amounts that come from specific individuals. I think of my financial rewards being an average of my high-paying clients and my favorite deadbeats. It all works out in the end.

kissing pavlov's dog's butt

Here's a phenomenon I've seen in Los Angeles:

You move here from a small town, and you realize there is money to be made. You've got skills. Talents. People wanna pay you. That's a good thing!

A year later, you find yourself busy and distracted from your own artistic sensibilities. Like Pavlov's Dog, you drool when someone wants to hire you and make you feel valuable. You jump through hoops, roll over, gimme paw and make your $100, then it's on to find some other idiot with the money.

If you cannot deal with failure, you cannot deal with success.

You do that enough times, becoming so dependent on them for your existence, that you forget what you even came here to do. You look back and realize you've become a tool for other people's bad ideas.

Promise yourself you won't be doing it forever. Always have an exit strategy. It can be tough to walk away from paid work, but sometimes you have to in order to claim your own creativity back.

beware of people with bad ideas and money

Sometimes you'll find a client who has seemingly unlimited financial resources. It's never clear how he got it. (Let's just assume he gets his money from cocaine smuggling.)

You'll probably find that working for him is impossible, because there's no connection between his goals and reality. He has no sense of workflow or efficiency.

When someone has worked his way up in the real world, he understands the value of time, energy, and people. He learns how to make good decisions. He learns about cause and effect. He learns about communication. He learns all sorts of things by making mistakes and suffering consequences.

Creatures who are mysteriously rich don't learn those lessons. When they encounter an obstacle, they get out what Robert Rodriguez calls "The Money Hose." (*Rebel Without A Crew*, 1996).

Spend enough time in that world, and your judgment will get worse. Bad ideas are contagious.

section 4:
your client sucks

warning signs

maybe they're cool, maybe they're not. Look out for the following:

1. **Referred by a Problem Client.** People tend to only perceive and meet other people who have the same problems that they have. It's uncanny. If you drop two losers into a room with a thousand successful people, you can bet the two losers will find each other.
2. **They call on the phone.** Bad sign. It means they're "people people" instead of "technical people." They want to run their mouth. It means you need to interpret what they say in real-time and write it all down for later. People who like to talk don't know what they want.
3. **They start their email with the words, "As per our conversation."** Corporate jive. Run as fast as you can in the other direction.
4. **They email you from their iPhone.** Prepare for confusion.

bad personality types

These people definitely suck.

The Hassler. Nothing is easy with this person. He'll call 15 times a day just to give you a hard time. This type of person wants to deal with you just for the sake of bossing someone around and having control. He'll walk all over you because he can.

The Haggler. This guy wants a discount, and will try to pressure you about it. He doesn't even NEED a discount. He just wants one. Doesn't work on me. I don't care about the money, and neither should my clients. I am happy to work for free for the right person. Trying to beat me down from my low hourly rate is cheesy and pointless.

The Poser. This person wants specific yet arbitrary things. Example: "We need a WordPress Page on the site [sic.] and we also want some Facebook Widgets." Huh? This type of client is an amateur who has hastily read a *Dummies* book and heard rumors about how their business works. They'll often learn some random "design rule" and then wonder what's wrong with you and why you don't follow it. Usually, they've inherited money, and they want to spend it. They're in and out of business in a month or two. Enjoy this black hole of buzzwords while it lasts.

The Hurrier. Watch out for people who falsely project a sense of urgency. They'll sometimes fake deadlines in order to get you to work faster. These people are typically very disorganized and pushy, and will call you at 11 p.m. on a holiday. They're desperate, and they tend to think that everything that ever happens to them is a once-in-a-lifetime opportunity.

The Compulsive Typer. Beware of people whose emails are full of witty prefaces, parentheticals, semicolons, postscripts, afterthoughts, follow-ups to follow-ups, and confirmations of confirmations. This is no joke: I once had a client who typed 6,675 words in regards to TWO MOCKUPS I did for his band's website. That's the equivalent of about 22 pages in this book you are holding. I would spend more time reading his emails than I would working. I want concise directions, Twitter-style. Bullet points.

> Release everything. It's the only way you'll know what works and what doesn't.

The Hustler. This guy is just plain dangerous, and you should get rid of him as soon as you can. He's always trying to sniff out some deal. He'll drag you into all sorts of schemes that you'll regret. He'll try to make some kind of "trade" with you, which will never be worth anything. He'll use you for everything you're worth and then it's on to the next party.

The Friend. This is a Haggler in disguise. He'll infiltrate your life and make you think he really understands you and likes you — as long as you keep working for free.

jargon and mr. pop, the emphasizer of everything

Mr. Helpless Client knows just enough design jargon to use it wrong. He doesn't know what words like Texture and Contrast really mean.

He has no experience, yet he's your boss!

You'll have to tell him: Texture is the difference between Carpet and Stone. If you ran your fingers over it, would the surface be rough? Smooth? Contrast is unlikeness or difference between two extremes. One object is big, another is small. One element is dark, another is light. In fact, these two are dependent on each other. On a computer screen, you need size variation. If you try to make everything big, everything will just look medium-sized. It's relative.

Compare your work to the best.

And when it comes to Typography, beware of Mr. Pop, The Emphasizer of Everything.

I've worked for him, more than once.

He wants every single word and image in the design to "pop" with equal significance.

Like the rock musicians in a studio: "Turn me up just a little bit?" They don't realize that there is a lead instrument at any given time, while the others provide support. They also haven't figured out that a loud part of the song is only loud if you also have a soft part before it/after it. When every instrument is already playing loud, how can you expect to get louder? You don't add five more guitar tracks, because that equals mud.

Back to Mr. Pop: He will also ask you to **bold** and *italicize* and underline every single word, because every bit of data he shovels onto the Internet is incredibly important.

Poor Mr. Pop.

You're going to need to interpret people and deal with their lack of education and vocabulary. It's your job to educate them. You've been doing this for a long time. They haven't.

all freelance clients are insane

People make decisions for strange reasons.

An example: You design a flyer for someone. You use all of your years of experience, you use your good taste, you do something to the best of your ability.

But they don't like *sans serif* typefaces.

What? WHY? *No one knows.*

Maybe you're designing an advertisement for a deep sea fishing boat, but the owner doesn't happen to like the color blue. Why? Maybe he was beaten up by a Smurf when he was a child. The guy just doesn't care that blue goes with water. His neurosis has taken over, and now you're stuck using red.

Face it, you're in a world full of insane people. People grow up with all sorts of hang-ups and fears.

Pretend that your job is to help the mentally handicapped.

Repeat the following Mantra: *"I work in a mental hospital. When he doesn't like green snake, I hide green snake."*

the return of the cargo cult

Be careful with First Drafts. People fear change and like what is familiar to them.

Even if it's a really bad idea, your client might cling to it because it's the first thing they saw. Somehow, they think that's how it was always supposed to be!

Sometimes you'll inherit a client from a horrible, amateur designer. And you'll be stuck copying that awful style sheet until the end of time. Why? Because the old designer is always better than you are.

Maybe you should have listened to the warning: "My old designer disappeared and won't return my calls."

The good news:
No one cares.
Enjoy the artistic
freedom of
obscurity!

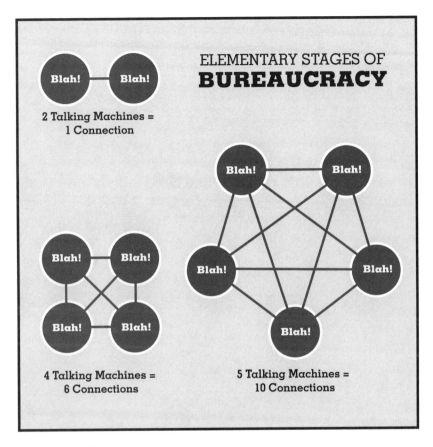

ELEMENTARY STAGES OF BUREAUCRACY

2 Talking Machines =
1 Connection

4 Talking Machines =
6 Connections

5 Talking Machines =
10 Connections

avoid bureaucracy

I stay the hell away from large companies.

The more people who work somewhere, the fewer there are who really know what is going on. Too many people need to sign off on things, there are too many policies, and it takes too long to communicate. Information doesn't flow freely enough to the people who are capable of making decisions or taking action.

If you can't work with a single individual, at least work with small companies where you can immediately get in touch with the people in charge. *Then just ignore everyone else.*

Two heads are better than one? No! In the Elementary Stages, we start out with two Talking Machines connected by a single Connection. Notice that at this starting point there are more Talking Machines than Connections. The Confusion increases exponentially from there — 10 Talking Machines are connected by *45 possible lines of communication*, as we see in the Advanced Stages.

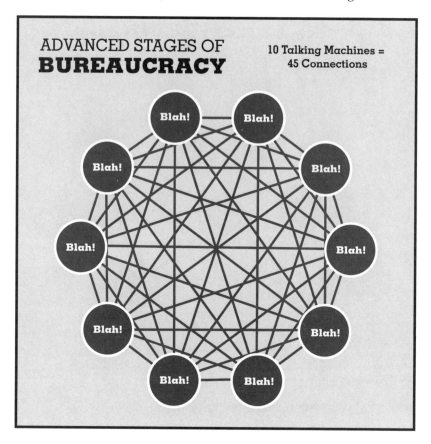

I politely turn down corporate clients.

how to fire a client

There comes a time when you have to "set someone sailing off, tears in their eyes," as Tamar Halpern once said. Maybe it's because they're just impossible to please, yet they won't go away. So here is what I do. Very simple:

> "Hi Client. I can't afford to take on any more work right now."

That's all it takes. It's polite, and it's true.

It's the old 29/71 Rule again. 29% of your clients will take up 71% of your time.

You'll be amazed at how much easier your life will be if you eliminate those energy vampires.

It's not that they're bad people. But let's face it, when we're selling our irreplaceable life essence (our time) we want to make the most money for doing the least amount of work.

"If you want roses, keep the weeds cut."
— Robert Ringer, Looking Out For #1

Remember: A client is *always* better off hiring someone who can share their dream. Maybe that's not you, and that's OK.

Art is not about competition, it's about expression.

Make the strong choice.

Now.

the final word

according to society's standards of success, creative people are typically ranked somewhere near the level of drug addicts and mental patients.

It's time to **kill that cliché**.

You can't afford to let your dream die.

You've got to find a way to make it exist in *the real world*.

If you're really serious — if you're willing to go *all the way* — that might mean living with no car, no TV, no family, no restaurants, no college degree, no savings, no vacations, no pets, no parties, no friends, and… *no massive comic collection*.

Is it worth it? Only *you* can decide.

For me, it was! I've successfully traded it all for one thing: a Creative Career. I've freed myself from the curse of being an employee at a 9-to-5 day job. I'm unencumbered. It's always been my dream to spend the majority of my time on my own creative projects, and now *I'm doing it*.

> Every creation needs a Seed, the central DNA that is present in every phase of its growth.

I can officially say I use my imagination for a living, working with some of my favorite musicians and artists. I help others achieve their dreams while funding my own.

This is a continuing, strange adventure. There will be new, confusing problems to solve, because that's what I signed up for. The journey is far from over. What will I do next? We'll see.

I've obsessively collected the strange philosophical ideas that appear in this book for twenty years. In high school, they said I was crazy... not only because of the bright green toothbrush I wore around my neck, or the jar of rotting apple juice in my bedroom that I named Leroy, but because of all that time I spent staring into space, begging the aliens to *please take me back home.*

I don't do work. I help cool people achieve their dreams.

It paid off. I'm back where I belong. Exploring outer space.

I'm honored to have shared all of this stuff with you. I hope you take these baffling ideas even further than I have.

If an antisocial, introverted kid from a retirement town in Florida can figure it out, so can you.

Carl King in his spaceship, age 7.

the
end

Wow. You've reached the end of the book. Now it's time for you to write the sequel.

(Don't make me come back here...)

"Keep doing nothing, and when nothing happens, don't be disappointed."
— Randi Rhodes, talk radio host ca. 1993

"It was only real because we said it was real."
— John Flansburgh, They Might Be Giants (*Gigantic*, 2003)

"Here's the secret. There are two things that you have to do. One of them is to not stop. And the other one is to keep going."
— Frank Zappa (Pennsylvania State Police interview, 1981)

The world needs Mutants.

acknowledgments

alphabetical thanks to:

Harry Cox Brand, Chewbode, Brian Compton, Stephen Cox, Brendan Davis, Charley Deppner, Anthony Garone, GuitarTricks, Tamar Halpern, Chris Higgins, Dr. Shahram Jacobs, M.D., Ian Koss, Steve Krugman, Eman Laerton, John and Cynthia La Grou, Dale Lewis, Stephen McCarthy, Dave Meros, Anders Mouridsen, Mump-Dase, Brad Murray, Lance Myers, My Eccentric Family, Belén Ortiz, James Pitts, Martin Pursley, Walter Rossmann and Imprint, Cristofer Sanders, Christopher Schlegel, Ruta Sepetys, Simon Said… (especially Brad Fries), W. Spoon, Trey Spruance, Flail Tenacious, Toontrack, Devin Townsend and Tracy Turner, Troll Music, Steve Vai, Victims Family, Roger Von Oech, Will Maier, Michael Wiese and Ken Lee at MWP.

Far beyond mere shovelers, these two specialized technical gurus made my life easy: Matt Barber (the editor who let me get away with telling The Truth) and William Morosi (for countering my biggest temper tantrum of 2010 with mature professionalism and flawless typography as always). Pray to EROEI that these Creative Geniuses are assigned to your book.

Beware of working with people who don't have a factory.

Everyone else who has ever made my life difficult…

…and Atari, who has loyally guarded my feet as I've worked for ten years.

research

t he following things blew my mind. All of them are inspirations for the Creative Career concept.

Books

- *The Book of the SubGenius* – The SubGenius Foundation
- *The Real Frank Zappa Book* – Frank Zappa
- *A Whack On The Side of the Head* – Roger von Oech
- *The Fountainhead* – Ayn Rand
- *Rebel Without A Crew* – Robert Rodriguez

Movies

- *American Movie*
- *The NeverEnding Story*
- *The Matrix*
- *Spider-Man 2*
- *Idiocracy*
- *Office Space*
- *Fight Club*

Lectures

- *On Being A Man* – David D'Angelo
- *Time Of Your Life* – Tony Robbins
- *Cultivating An Unshakable Character* – Jim Rohn

Musicians

- Ani DiFranco
- Steve Vai
- NoMeansNo
- Victims Family
- Kevin Gilbert

You cannot truly own anything in this world. You can only borrow it/rent it until you die.

about the author

Under the names Sir Millard Mulch and Dr. Zoltan Øbelisk, Carl King has recorded or performed with Devin Townsend, Marco Minnemann and Virgil Donati.

His 2005 album, *How To Sell The Whole F#@!ing Universe To Everybody... Once And For All!*, was co-released through Trey Spruance's Mimicry Records. It was named as one of the top musical moments of 2005 by *The San Francisco Bay Guardian*.

He is a pioneer drum programmer and is endorsed by Toontrack's *Drumkit From Hell* software.

Photo by Arkmay.

The highest and lowest points of his music career were having lunch with (and then failing an invite-only bass audition for) Steve Vai.

Carl has written for *mental_floss*, *INK19*, and *2600: The Hacker Quarterly*.

He lives in Los Angeles and has never owned a car.

Websites:

duckinalightbulb.com
bendbarsliftgates.com
carlkingcreative.com
drzoltan.com

All life is the story of change, from one state of being to another.

SAVE THE CAT!®
THE LAST BOOK ON SCREENWRITING YOU'LL EVER NEED!

BLAKE SNYDER

BEST SELLER

He's made millions of dollars selling screenplays to Hollywood and now screenwriter Blake Snyder tells all. "Save the Cat!®" is just one of Snyder's many ironclad rules for making your ideas more marketable and your script more satisfying – and saleable, including:

· The four elements of every winning logline.
· The seven immutable laws of screenplay physics.
· The 10 genres and why they're important to your movie.
· Why your Hero must serve your idea.
· Mastering the Beats.
· Mastering the Board to create the Perfect Beast.
· How to get back on track with ironclad and proven rules for script repair.

This ultimate insider's guide reveals the secrets that none dare admit, told by a show biz veteran who's proven that you can sell your script if you can save the cat.

"Imagine what would happen in a town where more writers approached screenwriting the way Blake suggests? My weekend read would dramatically improve, both in sellable/producible content and in discovering new writers who understand the craft of storytelling and can be hired on assignment for ideas we already have in house."
> – From the Foreword by Sheila Hanahan Taylor, Vice President, Development at Zide/Perry Entertainment, whose films include *American Pie, Cats and Dogs, Final Destination*

"One of the most comprehensive and insightful how-to's out there. Save the Cat!® *is a must-read for both the novice and the professional screenwriter."*
> – Todd Black, Producer, *The Pursuit of Happyness, The Weather Man, S.W.A.T, Alex and Emma, Antwone Fisher*

"Want to know how to be a successful writer in Hollywood? The answers are here. Blake Snyder has written an insider's book that's informative – and funny, too."
> – David Hoberman, Producer, *The Shaggy Dog* (2005), *Raising Helen, Walking Tall, Bringing Down the House, Monk* (TV)

BLAKE SNYDER, besides selling million-dollar scripts to both Disney and Spielberg, was one of Hollywood's most successful spec screenwriters. Blake's vision continues on *www.blakesnyder.com.*

$19.95 · 216 PAGES · ORDER NUMBER 34RLS · ISBN: 9781932907001

THE MYTH OF MWP

In a dark time, a light bringer came along, leading the curious and the frustrated to clarity and empowerment. It took the well-guarded secrets out of the hands of the few and made them available to all. It spread a spirit of openness and creative freedom, and built a storehouse of knowledge dedicated to the betterment of the arts.

The essence of the Michael Wiese Productions (MWP) is empowering people who have the burning desire to express themselves creatively. We help them realize their dreams by putting the tools in their hands. We demystify the sometimes secretive worlds of screenwriting, directing, acting, producing, film financing, and other media crafts.

By doing so, we hope to bring forth a realization of 'conscious media' which we define as being positively charged, emphasizing hope and affirming positive values like trust, cooperation, self-empowerment, freedom, and love. Grounded in the deep roots of myth, it aims to be healing both for those who make the art and those who encounter it. It hopes to be transformative for people, opening doors to new possibilities and pulling back veils to reveal hidden worlds.

MWP has built a storehouse of knowledge unequaled in the world, for no other publisher has so many titles on the media arts. Please visit www.mwp.com where you will find many free resources and a 25% discount on our books. Sign up and become part of the wider creative community!

Onward and upward,

Michael Wiese
Publisher/Filmmaker